The Glam Life

Uplevel everything in a fun way using glamour as your filter to the world

FIONA FERRIS

ISBN: 9798834315902
Imprint: Independently published

Other books by Fiona Ferris

Thirty Chic Days: *Practical inspiration for a beautiful life*

Thirty More Chic Days: *Creating an inspired mindset for a magical life*

Thirty Chic Days Vol. 3*: Nurturing a happy relationship, staying youthful, being your best self, and having a ton of fun at the same time*

Thirty Slim Days: *Create your slender and healthy life in a fun and enjoyable way*

Financially Chic: *Live a luxurious life on a budget, learn to love managing money, and grow your wealth*

How to be Chic in the Winter: *Living slim, happy and stylish during the cold season*

How to be Chic in the Summer: *Living well, keeping your cool and dressing stylishly when it's warm outside*

A Chic and Simple Christmas: *Celebrate the holiday season with ease and grace*

The Original 30 Chic Days Blog Series: *Be inspired by the online series that started it all*

30 Chic Days at Home: *Self-care tips for when you have to stay at home, or any other time when life is challenging*

The Chic Author: *Create your dream career and lifestyle, writing and self-publishing non-fiction books*

The Chic Closet*: Inspired ideas to develop your personal style, fall in love with your wardrobe, and bring back the joy in dressing yourself*

The Peaceful Life*: Slowing down, choosing happiness, nurturing your feminine self, and finding sanctuary in your home*

100 Ways *to Live a Luxurious Life on a Budget*

Loving Your Epic Small Life*: Thriving in your own style, being happy at home, and the art of exquisite self-care*

Contents

Chapter 1. *Why glamour?* 1

Chapter 2. *Choose a glittering vision for your life* 6

Chapter 3. *Cultivate a luxurious state of mind....* 14

Chapter 4. *Have an air of mystery* 21

Chapter 5. *Create a life full of vibrant rich health*
.... 29

Chapter 6. *A home environment of ease and elegance*..38

Chapter 7. *Beautify your space*............................46

Chapter 8. *Inspire dazzling confidence in yourself* 54

Chapter 9. *Dress for your dreams* 64

Chapter 10. *Create an at-home vacation-every-day feeling* 74

Chapter 11. *Cultivate beauty rituals* 84

Chapter 12. *Perform your own glow-up* 90

Chapter 13. *Be the elegant lady* 98

Chapter 14. *Live by your values* 105

Chapter 15. *Choose a seasonal lifestyle* 114

Chapter 16. *Engage your mind* 122

Chapter 17. *Dine luxuriously* 130

Chapter 18. *Be wealthy in all ways* 138

Chapter 19. *Adopt an apology-free lifestyle* 147

Chapter 20. *Your glam life starts now* 154

50 Ways to live your most glamorous life 159

About the author.. 169

Chapter 1.
Why glamour?

Why glamour? All I have to say is *Why not*? Why not choose a glamorous life over a mediocre existence? Why not have a little fun flavouring everything you do with pizzazz, sparkle or razzle dazzle (choose your favourite)? Life really is too short to settle for average when you have the option to approach all parts of your world through the lens of glamour instead.

Who said you have to be reasonable and normal and... boring?

Glamour is all about allure and mindset. When we choose to cloak ourselves in an attitude of glamour there is no telling how good things can get. Even when we still live the same life with the same lovely people in it, doing the same job and with the same resources. A personal definition of glamour for me would be making the best of everything regardless of my budget.

The beauty of glamour is that we can create it in lots of small ways, every day, for ourselves. We can bring a feeling of easy glamour into our life and the purpose of this book is to show you how.

Glamour is described as being more attractive, exciting, or interesting than ordinary people or things. Captivating, fascinating, beautiful and smart. Bewitching and enchanting. Who wouldn't want to be all this?

The effect glamour has on us is intoxicating

When you walk into a beautiful hotel or an elegant restaurant, all your senses are engaged. There is a feeling of excitement and specialness in the air. Even before you get there you have taken the time to look your best.

Why not carry this feeling through into an ordinary day by bringing a little more splendour and flair to how you show up?

Glamour is not reserved for the rare few. I believe any of us who wish to live a more fanciful life can invoke glamour into how we spend our time and how we interact with others. And it doesn't need to be silly or vapid either.

When we do things that light us up, everyone benefits. Our tasks are completed in an effortless manner. We are cheerier to anyone we come into contact with. We eat and spend mindlessly less often because we truly are enjoying the here and now. We don't go looking for fun in unhelpful places (overeating, overspending) because we are already having a great time living our amazing life!

Glamour is intentional

This is not something that just any one can have though because you do need to put in the effort. Living a glamorous life doesn't happen by accident. It is curated.

But the secret is, it's fun effort. It makes you want to jump out of bed in the morning. When you are feeling effortlessly motivated to go after your dream life and inspired to take action, it's easy. It's super good fun, and your enthusiasm will uplift those around you too. It's so worth it, which is the same of anything important in life really, don't you think? – being healthy, earning a living, or having good relationships with our loved ones.

So, are you willing to uplevel yourself?

The Glam Life will support you in enjoying your daily life and having more fun. It will teach you how to be happier. Living a glamorous life helps you deal with stress – truly! – and encourages you to enjoy your work. When you view your life through the iridescent lens of glamour anything is possible.

Come with me, take my hand and let my alter ego lead yours through the city streets together.

3

What does your glamorous counterpart look like? Mine holds a cigarette in one of those long black holders, and slowly bats her eyelashes at me when I'm contemplating being boringly normal versus glamorously bewitching. *Come on darling*, she drawls, *buck up*.

It's funny that I neither smoke nor wear false lashes, but that's just the image that comes to mind! Imagine you and I together boutique-hopping, as we skip through the coming pages. Such fun! I can't wait.

(And of course, I'm not saying that everyone needs to strive for a glamorous life. I get that it won't be a drawcard for a lot of... normal... people. But if what I'm saying rings your bell, welcome in!)

May this book bring you so much joy, fun and elegance, just by the virtue of you picking it up. May it infuse your thoughts and desires with happiness, a lustrous sparkle, and golden-tinted glamour,

xx Fiona

Your *Glam Life* tips:

Find yourself a pretty journal or notebook, or open Notes on your phone or a new Word document on your computer.

In this space, which will be *exclusively* to **dream of your glamorous life**, write down phrases or words from this book that resonate with you, any ideas which are sparked off as you read, and ponder answers to the inspirational questions at the end of each chapter.

I promise, by the time you finish this book you will have your own manifesto absolutely *brimming* with golden goodness.

Your *Glam Life* inspirational questions to contemplate:

~   *If you could choose anything you wanted and had no constraints at all, what kind of glam life would you want for yourself? What would it look like? What are elements that spring to mind immediately?*

~   *List the three main areas of your life and consider for each: What are ten simple things I could do in this category to bring a little glamour into it?*

Chapter 2.
Choose a glittering vision for your life

If I asked you to dream up glamour and describe it, you might talk about a person very flamboyant and old school. Elizabeth Taylor comes to mind for me, or someone equally over-the-top, dripping in huge jewels and wearing a silk caftan. Or perhaps 1950s era Sophia Loren in big sunglasses and a bombshell bikini.

But let's take it down to a more personal level, because we want to see how we can enhance *our* life, as it is right now. We want to create a compelling vision for our own version of a glam life.

Glamour can be anything that lends a flavour of luxury, feeling special, elegance and beauty. It elevates the everyday with its allure.

There are many nuances of glamour, and we can each choose what most speaks to us when we are deciding what to take in. Personally I love my simple life. The phrase 'a simple life' has always held something magical for me. I just love it! It feels peaceful and calming. In a simple life I get to relax, be creative, and just live.

A simple life might sound incompatible with a glamorous life, but that's the fun of dreaming – *you* get to decide the details, and how they all fit together too.

~ I like a simple life with touches of glamour.
~ I like to be savvy with my finances by living simply, and when we want to splash out that's okay too because we don't do it all the time.
~ My schedule is kept simple on purpose because it feels luxurious to me to have free time to create and 'be'.

An ordinary day infused with glamour

How would a normal day look for you if you amped it up a bit, and sprinkled it with gold glittery glamour powder that you'd ordered online?

I can imagine for me, that I'd get out of bed extra early, like today when I woke up at 5.15am and decided just to get up rather than try and sleep until 6am when my alarm goes off.

Getting up early is such a treat for me, I don't

know why. Yes, I know you're thinking I am some kind of a freak! But today I just ran with it, and snuck down to my office to do some delicious writing, the writing you are reading right now. It feels yummy to me to be creating as the sun comes up, if I could see it behind the atmospheric low cloud that surrounds the trees outside my office window.

Your start to an ordinary day infused with glamour might be a sleep-in, complete with satin eye mask of course! And perhaps a nicer robe. My current robe is thick white cotton. The luxurious part of this is that it's reasonably new and I wash it often, so it always feels 'five-star hotel'. Maybe taking a look at your sleepwear is one little upgrade that will support your vision.

Then, as you have breakfast you could ask, 'Does this feel like my glam life?' My breakfast today will be chopped fresh pineapple and pear, with yoghurt. On the top will be sliced almonds, freshly cracked walnuts and toasted coconut flakes. How good does that sound? In our house we call it our 'vacation breakfast', because we had a tropical version (pineapple and melon) on our Hawaiian honeymoon many years ago. It honestly feels very special and like we are on vacation when we have this breakfast! So yes, I would definitely have this breakfast in my glam life.

But in the past I couldn't have said that. In the past I ate stodgy white toast with butter for breakfast, and had basically very little nutrition at all. Which breakfast does it sound like the glamorous lady would choose?

It's a fun exercise to go through your 'everyday' in your mind and make notes on how you could make little changes to enhance your experience. Look at what you wear for each part of your day (and night), what and how you eat (Is there a candle on your dinner table? Or a rose in a bud vase?), how you hold yourself and how you speak. It's all on offer!

A day of out-and-out glamour

What about considering a whole day of luxurious living? What would you do? Would you like a massage? A mani-pedi? To have your hair done? Would you go out for lunch, dinner or both?

It's fun to dream of a completely decadent day, and who knows, one day you might actually do all those things on your list.

Of course it all depends on how much you have to spend, and needs to be in alignment with your financial goals as well. In my 'simple life with touches of glamour', worrying about my money situation because I have overspent is *not* in alignment.

But I do love doing special things, so I spend on some services, and do others myself.

~ I love massage, so I'll go to my favourite Thai massage place every once in a while. Apart from that I massage my feet every night before bed with fragranced body cream, and make sure to moisturize my whole body after showering each morning. I can also cajole my husband into giving me a backrub or foot rub while we are watching television together.

~ I enjoy facials, but very rarely pay and go to a beauty spa. However, I take my time cleansing my face at night and patting in facial oil afterwards. I exfoliate my face in the shower a few times each week. And I paint on a mud mask when I remember. Just thinking to myself about having a spa hour after dinner feels heavenly and there is zero cost, plus it is very relaxing to do before bed.

~ I love going for a pedicure – my regular lady does my nails so much better than I can, and her leg and foot massage is heavenly. But I enjoy doing my own fingernails as a preference.

~ I enjoy my hairdressing appointment, and get my highlights done very naturally so I only have to go every ten to twelve weeks.

~ I enjoy cooking luxurious and healthy meals at home mostly, but if we do go out, the restaurant will be nice, and we won't skimp.

~ Mostly we are at home, but when we do stay somewhere I like it to be elegant and high style, and we'll go out for cocktails and dinner while we are there. And, at home, I try to bring details in that make us feel like we are staying at a five-star hotel such as nice towels which are changed often, and keeping our main spaces tidy and 'arranged'.

One day recently my husband Paul had a Friday off work, so we booked lunch at a place we'd been wanting to try. After lunch, walking back to the car we decided to go for a stroll around the village, and I ended up buying a pair of shoes on sale. They were black pumps and had a very interesting heel. Honestly, I felt like that 'lady of leisure' type going out for lunch and cocktails, then shopping for shoes afterwards. It was fabulous!

And it wasn't as if we'd spent thousands. Sure, it cost more than my usual scrambled eggs at home, but that's what I do most of the time. I'd rather eat out once a month and do something like that, than buy my lunch every day like I used to.

Intention and expectation

Come to expect glamour *all the time*. Set your intention that yes, you will lead a more glamorous life from now on. Raise your standards and move in that direction. Have an attitude and mindset of glamour – expect it to increase in your life – and look for it everywhere!

Why shouldn't your life be a grand affair, and a flight of fancy? Keep this in your secret garden and let it flavour the way you dress, speak, act, dine and interact with others. Let it be your secret sauce that others wonder why they find you so delightfully alluring.

Let yourself dream about how good things can get!

Your *Glam Life* tips:

~ What is your vision? How could you imagine yourself living if you decided to **adopt 'glamour' as your guiding word**? Would it change how you ate? Dressed? Moved? Would your posture instantly improve as mine has just done thinking about this question?

~ What flavour is your ideal glamour? Are you thrifty glamour? Savvy glamour? Spendy glamour? Country rustic glamour? Over-the-top everything glamour? I don't mean in your real world right now, I mean the ideal amazing **future you who has everything she wants**. Ask her what her glamorous life is like and see what fun details she dreams up for you.

Your *Glam Life* inspirational questions to contemplate:

~   *What is the vision I have for my glamorous life?*

~   *What are all the influences that I want to infuse into my flavour of glamour?*

~   *Is my money situation up for some glamour upgrades, or do I need to be savvy with my choices right now?*

Chapter 3.

Cultivate a luxurious state of mind

Glamour is all about the 'extra' we can add into our life, but beneath that comes our foundation – a *mindset* of glamour and luxury. When we encourage our mindset in the direction we are drawn to, our wishes come easier. There are no barriers or resistance. We are not fighting internally between how we have been thinking in the past and how we want to be in the future. We can offer the ultimate in support to ourselves by firstly creating that vision of how our ideal life might look, then mentally stepping into it.

Glamour is a vibe. It's a mentality. It's an aura surrounding a person. It's about keeping your focus on beauty, enchantment and style no matter the area.

Imagine how confident you would feel if you

always carried with you a mindset of luxury, ease, and expectation? If you naturally considered yourself a woman with elegant boundaries?

I tend to think of this way of being as playful and creative. I'm more successful in creating what I want when I don't take anything too seriously. Naturally the practical things in life will be dealt with, but beyond that I'm careful not to hold too tightly onto thoughts and beliefs, so I can float lightly through life and not feel weighed down by my own rigidity.

Over time we can become surer of how we feel on any given topic, but does this serve us? Sometimes I wonder. I like becoming wiser and knowing myself more as I get older, but I want to remain flexible in my outlook as well.

I made the decision a while back to 'get younger as I get older', which includes focusing on good health and vibrant fitness, but also in the way I interact with the world. I want to be open to fresh possibilities and new ways of being. I sometimes forget this, but when I re-remember it feels wonderful. I would heartily recommend it!

Fall in love with your life

Open yourself up to more good by intentionally swooning over your life as it is right now. Bloom where you are planted, as they say, and make the best of everything in your current situation. Wishing you were somewhere else or someone else is not in your best interest. There is a great saying about only you can be the best you, and you will make a poor version of someone else (and vice versa).

I love to channel stylish people in different areas of my life, such as Aerin Lauder or Coco Chanel when I'm in the mood, but *I love being me*. I adore being Fiona! There are plenty of people who are better looking, have more money, are dressed in finer clothes, and live in a home that would make me cry with joy, but I don't care. I love being me. I love my home, how I dress, and how I live *because I chose to do that*. I chose to fall in love with my life, bloom where I'm planted, and be the best version of me. It's just more fun that way.

And I also enjoy upleveling regularly to feel new and sparkly. I do this by inspiring myself on a regular basis by watching feelgood movies, creating inspiration for myself in my journal, reading books (fiction, non-fiction, and glossy picture books) and making my life as pretty as it can be with the time and energy I am willing to expend, and with my current resources too.

When you are strong in yourself, no-one can cast doubt or make you second-guess yourself. When you are happy with who you are, you are unshakeable. You are magnetic to others. They sense your happy confidence, and it all starts with your mindset.

Think about a day when you wake up grumpy. I have those days too! Sometimes it's because I look out the window and it's cloudy and windy. Those days are never inspiring. But then I give myself a shake. I get to create my own existence! Why am I giving my power over to *the weather*? Or another person if they wake up grumpy? Or an email if I check my phone and see that I have missed the deadline to choose my meals for the meal kit delivery company and they are sending me the default meals which include pork and I don't eat pork?

Yes, in that last case I was a bit grumpy with myself for not being more organized, but it is nothing that is too permanent. And funnily enough I had just said to my husband Paul a few months ago that perhaps I would start eating pork, just to be more flexible and open to new things rather than a blanket statement of, 'I don't eat pork' just because I've never fancied it. I certainly got what I asked for in a funny way!

When you fall in love with your life and create a feeling of romance in everything you do, nothing can get you down for long. Not the weather, not the mood of a loved one, or even a wrong order. Of course, sad situations happen in life that we cannot control, but when you have a zest for life and always look on the bright side, you are starting from a high point anyway. You are better able to handle difficult times from this vantage.

Keep glamour in mind

Find pure enjoyment in every moment no matter what you are doing, by bringing flair and finesse to the task. Do *everything* from a glamorous state of mind! This might look like:

~ Washing the dishes or chopping vegetables with something fabulous to listen to – an audiobook, movie, or your favourite music.

~ Setting the table with care and specialness for an ordinary weeknight dinner. Candles on a Tuesday? Of course!

~ Looking the best you can appropriate to the occasion, whether it's working from home, visiting a friend, or going out for dinner. A comfortable, stylish, practical outfit, a little makeup, hair tidy and a spritz of fragrance.

~ Adding the finishing touches such as sunglasses or a scarf (I forget more often than I remember these two things and they make a huge difference to looking and feeling more glamorous).

~ When you are out, channelling a word such as *charisma*, *mystique*, or *allure*. Letting it scent your mind.

~ Keeping perfumed handcream, an essential oil roller-ball and extra-soft tissues on your work desk – little luxuries that lift your spirit when you use them throughout the day.

We can transcend the ordinary and feel enchanted simply by changing our mindset. We can fascinate ourselves and others. When we hang glamour up as our backdrop, we have a beautiful, genuine smile on our face without even realizing it. We're having fun, in our own graceful way.

Cultivate your own state of mind and see how much things change!

Your *Glam Life* tips:

~   Decide today to **be the person you've always dreamed of being**. Be that girl who has high standards for herself. Cultivate charisma and a magical quality about yourself by filling your mind with all that is beautiful. Cast a spell over yourself by the way you view the world.

~   Remember glamour is not just about the way you look, it's about having the **confidence to face any situation with style and grace**. Wear an aura like a crown on your head, and if it gets knocked off somehow, simply pick it up and put it back on. Imagine entering a room with that thought in mind! You can't help but have an amazing time.

~   Elegance is being beautiful both inside and out. Think simple, pure, kind thoughts and let love flow behind you as if a wake in the ocean. Spread flowers of happiness by the way you are. Watch how alluring you come across to other people, and yourself as well! It's almost like a secret that **once you know it, you can't go back to the way you were before**. And before you knew it, you had no idea it was there.

~ Life is good. Life is wonderful. Remember that and build your mindset with a sense of peacefulness and delight. You are living in a fantasy world, a fairy tale, and **you get to take that with you into the real world**.

Your *Glam Life* inspirational questions to contemplate:

~ *How is my current mindset holding me back from creating the way I would love to live?*

~ *What are some beliefs I'd like to change to make me more excited about life?*

~ *What are some simple ways that I can practice those thoughts? (i.e. if you'd like to believe that life is a magical mystery unfolding perfectly in an imperfect world, decide that and see what flows from there).*

~ *Create a list of your most unfavourite tasks and see how you can glam them up. Go through all your senses as prompts.*

Chapter 4.

Have an air of mystery

One of the quickest and easiest things you can do to bring a little more glamour into your life, is to cultivate your mystique. Become someone that, when they speak, others are leaning in to hear what they have to say.

Glamour is not someone spilling their guts or letting it all hang out. Oversharing is not a captivating trait! Yes, we want to be truthful and transparent with those who are important to us, but I think it's a forgotten virtue to simply smile and say nothing sometimes. I know I have spoken many times simply to fill the air, and really, who wants to listen to that? And the regret afterwards can be brutal as you recall to yourself how you couldn't shut your mouth for love or money.

When you set the intention to be more mindful

with what you say, it becomes a fun practice to think for a minute how something is going to sound before it comes out. Sometimes that filter slips out of place, and you have to think to click it back in again. My filter is notoriously faulty a lot of the time so it's a constant focus for me to not be that torn sack going blah blah blah.

I like to pretend I'm in a movie scene sometimes. Maybe the scene is set in a coffee shop and the main character (me!) is meeting a friend. I'll glide up to the counter, order my coffee pleasantly and sit down – with good posture of course! I will make conversation with my friend by asking interesting questions and making sure I don't dominate the conversation.

I know it all sounds a bit premeditated, but some of us who come from a long family line of talkers has to always be on guard!

The golden hallowed thought of being an elegant lady sipping her drink and partaking in delightful conversation is what keeps me happy. I want to leave a social situation with happy thoughts, not remorse. And when you use your ears and mouth in the proportion in which they have been given to you, it's almost a guarantee to happen, thank goodness.

Keep your plans in your secret garden

The movie 'Dream House' features Daniel Craig playing a writer. In one scene his wife asks him, 'Are you going to tell me what your new novel's all about?'

and he replies, 'If I tell you about it, then it all just disappears.'

This is exactly what happens to me with an exciting book idea too. In fact, when the idea for *The Glam Life* come to me, I was so excited. I had this vision of a fabulous book about living your most glamorous life all by the way you viewed things – no money needed to be spent, you could still keep your family and still live in the same home. I was pumped with ideas!

I furiously tapped out notes in my phone in a waiting room. Then, when I got home I copied and pasted those notes into a document on my desktop computer and added to them. I never breathed a word of the topic or the fact I had started writing a new book to anyone, not even my husband, because I knew from previous situations when I had done that all the excitement came out. It's definitely a real thing!

And in normal people non-writer's land it's true too – have you ever had an idea for a project at work or at home and felt so full of good energy about it but then shared your thoughts with someone else, sometimes within the minute? Firstly, they may not see it the same way you do, or it may not be a passion of theirs like it is yours. And secondly, you've let the idea out, like air from a balloon. And we all know what you're left with when you let the air go from a balloon!

So please, I beg of you, next time you have a brainwave that knocks you off your feet with its utter coolness, keep that idea safe and coddled while you work on it. Keep it in your secret garden and resist the urge to share with anyone who will listen. Nurture it and let it blossom until you can't keep it under wraps any longer (preferably when it's finished or near completion).

Move in silence

Similar to having a secret garden for your dreams and goals is the current trendy phrase to 'move in silence'. When I first heard it I *loved* it. To me, moving in silence means making plans and carrying them out *then* telling people about them (or not even then).

Take weight loss and getting healthier as an example. I know, it's so thrilling to latch onto a new, enticing plan or join an online fitness app and be so amped about the changes you are going to make. You tell your mother, your sister, and your best friend. You tell your husband that night that you are going to be making some big changes in your life.

Fast forward one week and you've forgotten all about your excitement for getting slimmer when you are having chocolate cravings and enjoying a cozy night on the sofa with a romantic comedy and a large bar of milk chocolate (with ice cream in the freezer for afters).

But those people you told probably haven't forgotten. No, you can imagine them thinking, 'That Fiona, she never follows through'. Urgh, no no no, let's rewind.

Instead let's picture the following. You get the thought in your head that you want to be different going forward. You are going to flick a switch and be a new person. You are going to fit into your clothes that are hanging sadly unused in your closet thanks to comfort eating and hormonal changes in your body. It's no fun feeling like a loser who can't fit her clothes anymore, so you are going to make some changes!

Important step: You commit to not breathing a word of this to anyone!

You then set about making small changes in the key areas where you know you are not honouring yourself. You write down the danger points in your day and work out ways to lessen the damage. You know that you collapse in the door after work famished and eat whatever is easy and yum. You know that you fall into a glass of wine before dinner.

So, perhaps eating lunch later and dinner earlier could be a plan? Having dinner prepped the night before so that when you come home it's all there ready to cook and you do this before your brain even gets a chance to derail you?

Then, you journal to yourself how fabulous it's going to be when you can reach into your closet and pull out absolutely anything to wear. It's going to be amazing! You visualize how good you're going to look in your favourite jeans and that silky top, and you imagine heads turning when you wear it again. You look forward to social occasions instead of dreading them, because you know people are going to say, 'You look fab! Love that dress!'

Not telling people your plans, making small changes to your routine and diet, and visualizing your future success are all easily doable things you can start when you decide to move in silence.

It's the same with writing a book. Perhaps you have dreamed of being an author for a long time but never got the traction. Your family is tired of hearing how you are going to write a book 'one day'. Imagine instead if you snuck in half an hour each day and worked on your book. And not tell a single soul about it. You would keep it hugged to your chest like a secret. It's just you and the book inside this cozy little incubation space. You are in a beautiful magical chrysalis!

Keep on going, keep on going, keep on going, whether it's with your health goals or writing your book. Don't tell anyone and keep on going.

Then, one day, you will debut your jeans that you haven't fitted for six years. You will upload your book to Amazon for sale. You will lay that quilt you have been working on at the end of your guest bed. You will serve the dish of macarons you have been practicing making, at your lady friends afternoon tea. (See I added a few extras in there?)

There is no end to what you can achieve, and also with a degree of mystique, charm and mystery when you speak less than might feel normal, whether it's in a social situation or to do with your exciting plans. Just remember, a smile is always welcome and often all you need!

Your *Glam Life* tips:

~ **Remember your allure** when you are tempted to overtalk in a situation. You are a woman with mystique and you want people to look forward to seeing you, not go running in the other direction.

~ **Cultivate your secret garden** and plant beautiful wishes in there. Tend them and bring them to light once they are completed.

~ **Show people what you can achieve** rather than telling them. It's so much more satisfying!

~ Even in your relationship – *especially* in your relationship, **keep your mystique**. Even if you haven't in the past. You can change! Simply decide that from today, *I will not let it all hang out. I will talk about things less and simply be me, with more mystery.*

Your *Glam Life* inspirational questions to contemplate:

~   *How can I act in social situations to be in alignment with the woman I imagine myself to be?*

~   *What do I want to keep in my secret garden? What belongs in my journal to nurture and grow rather than blab out to everyone?*

~   *What are my greatest goals and dreams that I would be so happy to achieve, and which one will I choose first to 'move in silence' with?*

Chapter 5.
Create a life full of vibrant rich health

When I wanted to uplevel my health, both for now to look and feel better in my clothes, and the future me as a fit, energetic retiree one day, I changed the way I viewed 'healthy living'.

In the past it was quite a chore to choose the healthy choice, to not have fun eating and drinking everything I wanted and never saying no to myself. It seemed too boring to have discipline and do things in moderation. Perhaps you can relate?

But when I changed my angle from choosing a healthy lifestyle to a glamorous lifestyle, everything changed. When I changed from cooking a healthy meal to the way a wealthy, elegant lady would dine, a whole new world of inspiration opened up to me.

Think about those glamorous, rich ladies who swan around on launches on the French Riviera, dressed in fabulous palazzo pants, wearing a silk Hermès scarf around their head, and big shiny black sunglasses. Okay, so that might just be on Pinterest and in the movies; I've never been to the South coast of France. But I'm sure they exist!

Do you think they look like that by chowing down on French fries and gallons of ice cream? No, me neither. I think they look like that because they have fresh fruit and yoghurt for breakfast, served on the terrace by their staff, of course. They might order a Caesar salad for lunch with a goblet of sparkling mineral water. And they might have their private chef serve them up fresh fish cooked in butter and lemon juice for dinner, with a side of roasted asparagus and a chilled Chablis.

That is what motivates me to cook more elegant food – ***the glamour lens*** – and of viewing my life as an inspiring movie or photo shoot. Glamorous, wealthy people look good. They are trim and vibrant. There will be unhealthy people who live that lifestyle for sure, but I would say overall they look better than us 'normal' people!

Being 'normal' doesn't need to stop us from looking as good as we can though, and it all starts with how we fuel our body. It's easier to feel glamorous when our health is not being degraded by unwise choices.

Plan for your Riviera-style success

Having a rich rockin' body doesn't require expensive surgery or a full-time personal trainer. We can do it for ourselves by making the best selection every time we are facing a decision. I often find it easier to make decisions in advance; it gives me a better chance of making the right choice.

For example, my husband Paul and I planned to go out for Sunday lunch. Often we will have a glass of wine with our meal when we do this, but I had decided I didn't want any alcohol that day. A glass of wine at lunch can leave me feeling tired in the afternoon, so I planned on having sparkling water instead, and would ask the staff for a few slices of lemon in my glass.

I also pre-thought my food – I was going to have the pan-fried fish and salad, with no French fries. I stuck with my plan, even though Paul was having a beer with his lunch and it would have been pleasant to have a glass of wine with my fish. Not only was I proud of myself for following through on my healthy-glamorous-life plan, I had a lovely afternoon also, without that tired feeling.

And it's the same with exercise, I had planned to go for a one-hour walk in the morning before we went out for lunch, and I did.

Making as many healthy choices as we can in any given moment means the momentum – and results – build up, and the cumulative effect over time uplevels our health and fitness. We also get to feel good in ourselves in the current moment because we have acted in alignment with the person we want ourselves to be.

Look to your future

Another powerfully motivating force is to fast-forward into the future. Do you want to be someone who has a complicated lifestyle because of poor health decisions in the past? No, you want to be healthy, vibrant and enjoying yourself.

I imagine myself as a retiree in the next twenty years *having the time of my life*. Travelling, loving life, and feeling happy at the end of each day because I spent that day exactly how I imaged I would in my perfect, ideal life. And that idyllic existence starts with how I am today.

I'm sure I am not alone when I think to myself, 'Well, I will be that healthy person in the future, dancing around all slim and svelte, with tons of sparkly energy, but right now I feel like chocolate, so I'm just going to go ahead and eat it'.

But when we think like this, tomorrow never comes. The next day when we wake up it's 'today' again. A day in which we get to choose how we want to fuel our body. If we choose food and drink that does not align with the healthy, optimistic future vision we have for ourselves, we are turning away from our wishes once more, and our health slides infinitesimally downhill day by day.

And we can just as easily raise our health score

day by day by doing the opposite – planning out our ultimate day of food and drink, and simply following through with our initial desires.

The cool thing to know is that healthy choices are often just as easy to make as unhealthy choices, it's just that we *think* we feel like the unhealthy option more. But when we fast forward to afterwards, we realize, 'Oh, I forgot there were consequences. I actually feel really yucky after eating all that popcorn.'

When we act in alignment with our *goals* and not our *feelings*, we always make a better choice. And sometimes it's just the act of remembering our desires and putting them ahead of a fleeting craving or impulse. So simple and yes it can be easy! Hoorah!

Get the rich girl glow

Something else that differentiates us mere mortals from those glamorous jet-setting types is a glowing complexion. This can be brought about by good skincare, facial treatments, and the excellent light-handed application of a combination of bronzer and highlighter. Another contributor is slightly vigorous exercise which induces a sheeny dew to the skin and good blood circulation which brightens your face.

You can imagine that the rarefied trust-fund lady has a regular regime of walking, yoga and Pilates. She might do ballet barre or work out with light weights. We can do this too! We can go for a walk, attend a yoga class or follow online, or learn dance moves from a YouTube video.

Whatever is enjoyable and most importantly the least excuse producing for you, decide to do that daily. Be that glamorous lady working out to look and feel her best.

Just as with choosing to think of healthy eating as *glamorous eating* to make it more exciting, so too decide to rebrand for yourself the word exercise. Choose to see it instead as *glowy movement, your elegant practice, enhancing your beauty,* or *physical vitality.*

Dress the part in long black leggings and a fitted black top and be the wealthy lady working out. Picture yourself gaining a rich girl glow and it will be no problem to look forward to gentle body movement each day.

Have exquisite posture

And finally, what can we do in an instant to look taller, slimmer, more glamorous and like someone who values and takes care of herself? We stand up straight, pull our shoulders back and have beautiful posture as if we were an off-duty ballerina. Think of Audrey Hepburn in any of her movies – her back is straight and her posture perfection.

Some of us with a bigger bust do not want to flaunt it, I know that's why I don't always pull my shoulders down and back. But we are not making the most of our physique when we hunch, even if slightly. There is a subtle difference you can make when you push your shoulders back which means your posture is good and your bust not too pushed out and that is to curve your tailbone under slightly or tuck your bum in. Try it and you will see and feel the difference. Doing this also helps with lower back pain, especially when sitting down.

All the points in this chapter – healthy eating, glowy exercise and good posture – are not just superficial desires to look better. Yes, that's our lure, but what we are really gaining for ourselves is superb health, ongoing. The glamour aspect is what makes all our cumulative habits easy to do, and lifelong good health is the ultimate reward.

We can't control everything of course, life will throw us curveballs every now and then – some big, some small, and some major bombshells. But if we are in better health we are more prepared for it, both physically and mentally.

There really is no downside to being in the best health we can, and there is no need for anything to be boring, nor for you to feel like something is a chore. I want you to go out there and enjoy creating a life full of vibrant and rich health!

Your *Glam Life* tips:

Find your sticky areas with food and drink and brainstorm ways to make them healthier and more glamorous.

One for me is that I wanted to have plenty of alcohol-free nights each week, to sleep well, wake refreshed, and slim down easily. I decided on a couple of inspired actions:

1. To make a glass pitcher of fresh lemon slices and juice, plus a few sprigs of mint from the garden, and topped with sparkling water. I kept this in the fridge and poured into a champagne flute as an aperitif.

2. To decide for the time being to be a 'social drinker', that is to save alcohol for when we are with friends or out for dinner, and sip non-alcoholic drinks when we are at home.

And food-wise, I went back to a previous plan that worked well, and that is to only keep food in the house that the slim, chic, elegant me would eat. I would say no to unhealthy, non-glamorous food such as potato chips, candy etc when I was at the supermarket. When I saw them I would say to myself 'Slim and glamorous' and turn away. Then, when I am at home I don't need to try to resist them. It is so much easier to avoid snack foods when they are on a supermarket shelf and not my pantry shelf.

Rebrand exercise for yourself into something that you happily do most days. What have you enjoyed in the past and how can you get that excitement back?

Commit to excellent posture and even place a sticky note on your computer monitor to prompt you until it becomes automatic. Or maybe recurring reminders on your phone? Do whatever it takes to cement in that Audrey Hepburn mindset!

Your *Glam Life* inspirational questions to contemplate:

~   *How can I live a more glamorous life in the category of food and drink?*

~   *What items do I want to delete and what could I replace them with?*

~   *What kind of luxurious physical movement can I imagine the future me doing?*

~   *How can I get my rich girl glow?*

Chapter 6.

A home environment of ease and elegance

As you open the door to your hotel room on the first day of vacation you breathe a big sigh of relief while you scan the room. You put your bags down. You're here!

It's so peaceful. The room is clean, neat, and luxuriously appointed. You can feel yourself instantly unwinding because there is nothing to do except relax and enjoy yourself. Nothing to tidy or clean. No meals to make. You are completely taken care of in this moment.

And you, the traveller, have brought with you only a limited number of items dictated by the size of your suitcase. You packed only the best, nicest, and most favourite of what you own. You have curated the possessions you are going to live with on this trip and it's a pleasure to put those clothes away in the drawers and closet, set out toiletries in the bathroom, and place your Kindle by the bed.

Within a few moments your suitcase is empty, and it's stowed away leaving you to ask yourself, 'What do I want to do now?'

Wouldn't it be amazing if our whole life was like this? Wouldn't it be fabulous if there was as little admin to do at home as there is in a hotel room?

For most people, and certainly me, I never thought to live in a more streamlined and luxurious way because I suppose I just never thought to be different. I never considered that there was the possibility of joining these two sides of me. The one side who swooned in relaxed happiness – whether in real life or seeing a magazine image – at the sight of a highly simplified staged home or hotel room. And the other side – my own reality – of living in a home that always had lots of 'things' tucked away everywhere.

Most of us just never thought to consciously aim for that minimal home goal, and we still don't want an 'empty' home, but perhaps we could make some intentional edits to bring about a sense of ease and luxury.

It's difficult to feel like the glamorous woman you desire to be when you are frazzled and behind on *everything*. When your home life feels out-of-control I doubt you will float around with a relaxed disposition. It's hard to feel high-vibe and gorgeous when the house is a dirty mess. When you're running late and can't find your phone, you're less likely to feel like a glamorous film star featuring in the movie of your life.

Imagine instead if your home was neat and organized. You had everything laid out that you wanted to take with you that day. Your closet was tidy, and your clothes were hanging up clean and in good order, all ready to wear. Would you feel calmer and move in an elegant fashion in this serene world? Would you remember the star that you are and move languidly and with ease?

Think about that sense of peace you feel when you walk into a fresh hotel room, where everything has been taken care of for you. Why not do this for yourself at home by decluttering, organizing, and beautifying your space? *This*, I believe, is the foundation to living a glamorous life.

Closing the loop

There are always new items coming into our home just about every single day when you think about it – groceries, clothing, household essentials as well as larger purchases. But unless we are intentional about regular cleanouts, there is not always the equal number of possessions leaving our home.

We buy groceries, but are we using up the food we already have? We buy new clothes, but is this because an item needs replacing or did we spot something enticing and just had to have it?

It's easier when something is broken and unrepairable or just completely worn out, but it's not so simple for other things.

Recently I bought a few new sets of bath towels, and some gym leggings and sports socks for myself. With the towels, we had some which were looking tired. And with my leggings and socks, I've been walking every day on our treadmill and would run out of these two things between laundry days.

The step I was often missing in instances such as these, was to move along the extra, older items if I had any. The leggings were easy, no decluttering required because I didn't have enough pairs. But the socks, I needed to throw a few pairs out because they had lost their elasticity. And the towels, I needed to move the tired towels to gym towels for my husband Paul, and the current gym towels will go to cleaning towels or the SPCA if we have enough cleaning towels.

These few examples of closing the loop are just one small part of our home. And if we are busy or distracted and don't move along or clear out the items we replace, we can end up with cupboards, drawers and closets packed with too many things and we feel stressed out and unhappy with our home.

Arrange your life for glamour

As you declutter areas of your home you will notice how pleasing these spaces feel once they are organized neatly. And how easy it is to access what you need. Imagine if your whole home was simplified and tidied and felt this way too.

The old saying 'a place for everything and everything in its place' is so inspiring to me and is my personal goal for our home. I can envision how good it will feel to have that be true. There will be enough space for everything, I'll know where to look for anything I need, and there will be no wasted time spent searching through clutter for what I want.

Being uber-organized in your environment will pay dividends in how you feel in your home every day. Organizing and beautifying your home will centre you and help you feel amazing. When you tidy a space, instead of it constantly bothering you it is now a delight to go into that area – such as your closet.

Most of us lead a busy life, and our home needs to run well so that we don't become a frazzled, unglamorous mess. It might feel like an impossible task, but it can be done. Even if you have tons going on, there will be small changes such as tidying up a main hotspot so that you don't feel drained every time you walk past it. How nice will it be to be able to find the things you need when you need them! You will have a wonderful feeling of *Winning at Life!* when you lessen the friction in daily living.

Find routines that suit you

For a long time I didn't have a set day to go to the supermarket. I'd try to wait as long as possible and see what I could use up or I'd shop multiple times per week. There was no routine.

When I decided that yes, every Monday I was going to purchase what we needed for just one week, I instantly felt more relaxed. I didn't need to stock up too much on food and household items because I knew I only had to get through to Monday.

And it was the same with my laundry. I now aim to do one load of laundry most days, even if it's only a small load. I'll check my laundry basket in the morning and if there is enough for at least a half-load (our washing machine is huge), I'll put it on.

Compare this to my prior tactic which was to wait until I had a full load of lights, darks, or towels etc. I wanted to be greener and save money. I'm still all about both of those things, but I always felt like I had a mountain of laundry. Doing regular loads helps me feel in control and calm, and we always have clean clothes to wear.

Household admin and organization is unglamorous and unsexy but it leads to a more luxurious experience overall. When it is neglected is when we feel weighed down by the heaviness of things undone. This feeling does not lend itself to a glamorous life.

Make your home a haven that helps you feel surrounded by comfort, ease, and beauty. It can help buffer the outside world when you come back to your own space. When you come home to a place that meets your needs and takes stuff off your plate because it is clean, calm, and organized you can relax.

Focusing on making sure your home is running well means you may even get more time to spend on yourself. You will be able to enjoy a book with your feet up and a cold drink like you imagine your ideal glamorous self doing, without guilt because you don't have lots of tiny jobs hanging over you.

This to me is as good a reason as any to be more organized and regularly declutter and tidy my home. What a payoff – being able to live a luxurious life of peace, ease, and comfort.

Your *Glam Life* tips:

~   **Find a mental visual that inspires you** to clean up your home. Is it a hotel room? Model home? Minimal rooms online? Whatever that shining beacon is for you, keep it in mind and go through the rooms and spaces in your home, making them as enticing as you can.

~   **Compile a list of pesky undone tasks**. Empty your head of everything that is hanging over you. (When I did this, I realized that some of the items listed had been on my mental list for *years*!) Then, work through these tasks, starting with quick wins and the most bothersome. You will be amazed at how much better you feel after just a few. Imagine how good you will feel when you cross off this list in its entirety. And you can always delete some as unnecessary if you decide you don't want to move forward with them anymore. Deleting a task is a perfectly valid way of dealing with it.

~ **Consider adding routines into your life** that help deal with sticky areas – those parts of your day that always trip you up.

Your *Glam Life* inspirational questions to contemplate:

~ *How can I feel more glamorous in my home?*

~ *What would my home ideally feel like?*

~ *What are some items I would declutter immediately if I could guarantee no-one's feelings would be hurt?*

~ *Could I actually get rid of those items for real? How could I do that?*

~ *How could I live a luxurious life in the home I live in right now? What would have to change?*

Chapter 7.
Beautify your space

A major part of how we feel – glamorous or otherwise – is influenced by the environment we place ourselves in. Many of us spend a lot of time in our home and it is important to us, whether we work outside the home or not. Every single little thing we surround ourselves with will influence how we feel, and this is the most important thing, because how we feel will dictate how we behave.

Whether I have an unproductive day or a whizz-bang-finished satisfying day all comes down to how I woke up in the morning and what I chose to do with my time and energy that day. Yes, it comes from internal enthusiasm (or otherwise), but it is also majorly influenced by our living space, if it is a place that lifts us up versus drags us down.

For me a beautiful living space with all my favourite things around me is my personal definition of glamour. It can be easy to feel *laissez-faire* about your home when you've been there a while; that's why moving house is a great time to dream of your ideal vision. Stressful, but a fresh start.

I did that we when we moved house – I had a vision for our home. A glittery unrealistic vision for sure, but a nice little snapshot in my mind that I would have loved to fulfil.

I'm not all the way there yet, but slowly over the past four years we have made steps towards bringing that vision to life, and we still have a long wishlist of projects that we will do one or two of each year. Some are big and some more easily achievable. Some require significant funds and hiring trades people, but there is plenty on my list that I can do myself, with intention and focus.

That's when I saw that you don't need to move house to start afresh. You can look around with new eyes today, and start a wishlist to step towards. And, the great thing is that there will be plenty of little things you can do today, for free, that will make a huge difference to how you feel in your home. Glam life, here we come!

Make your home into your dream home

What comes to mind when you think of your dream home? Mine would be a rich, romantic cave of mystery and elegance, full of gold and reflective surfaces, with luxurious textures and cozy fabrics. I love patterned carpets and imagine my dream home would be a symphony for the senses. My ideal collab would be Ralph Lauren Home X French Chateau style X the Aerin brand.

I know, it's quite the scene! So how have I started bringing this vision into my reality, with ease and fun, and on a budget too?

When we moved into our house it was very normal, with off-white walls in every room and the same beige carpet throughout. On the advice of a friend who is an interior decorator, we focused on one room at a time. Her reasoning was that you start with one room and then let that inform the next room, and the next. It makes total sense!

We started with the living room and after showing her Ralph Lauren English country images I'd kept from magazines, we chose a rich deep navy/green/grey shade for the walls, and ordered antique-white linen curtains. I started looking for second-hand Persian rugs and bought a few inexpensively at a local auction house, as well as old paintings to create a gallery wall with. I found interesting inexpensive fabrics and made pillow covers to create that arty sofa look.

I always kept in mind my ideal collab when doing all these things, and it worked so well I still can't believe it. In this particular room, the living room, it was more the Ralph Lauren end of the spectrum, whereas when we started doing our bedroom, it swayed more Aerin and French Chateau. But starting out with an overall ideal vision in mind kept the flow cohesive from room to room.

Add to the ambience

Even if decorating is not in the budget, you can still do a lot with decluttering that room of non-ideal items, bringing in small or free changes (such as moving in items from another room) and creating an air of the feeling you want to create.

Another home feeling I like to create is a smoky, sultry jazz club in 1950s Paris. In the late afternoon I light candles and switch on LED candles. I turn off the main overhead lights and only keep on the lamps and wall lighting.

I'll change the music from the peaceful piano background music I like to play during the day to something sexier and more stylish for the evening.

Something I have found works well is to search for playlists on Spotify using words such as glamour, luxury, elegant etc. Brand names bring up great playlists too – Ralph Lauren, Starbucks and various hotels have yielded a bounty of music I enjoy. And there is just something about a playlist made by someone else – there is always that element of surprise because you never know what is coming next. I love that!

Even if you don't change the décor of your home at all, you can do a lot with ambience. Have you ever seen a bar or nightclub during the day? It's completely different and actually very disappointing and you immediately realize how much can be achieved with lighting and music – and mirrored surfaces!

Take a leaf out of their book and look for ways you can create your desired feeling at home: simply, quickly and inexpensively.

The culture of your home

Deciding on purpose what the culture of your home could be is a fun thing to think about. Imagine cultivating a specific energy, enriching routines, personalized rituals and generally making your home your sanctuary, your temple. And you the divine goddess who dwells within! Making your home as special and as sacred as you can will create such an alluring atmosphere that anyone who visits, as well as those who live with you, will feel how rare and unique this is.

You could even go so far as to write a manifesto or a list of guiding words on how you want the culture of your home to be. Some of the words to inspire the culture of my home are:

~ Serene, calm and peaceful
~ Orderly
~ An elegant country retreat
~ Luxurious, spa-like
~ Simple
~ Creative

~ Comfortable, cozy, enveloping
~ An oasis to restore equilibrium

To achieve this, and keep our home like this going forward, I have decluttered, tidied, and created storage solutions that are aesthetically pleasing as well as being easy to use.

I have chosen furniture that aligned with my desired look and feelings. I do the finishing touches every week such as fresh flowers in a vase from the supermarket, and rotating my glossy picture books for use as a plinth with a decorative candle on top.

Borrowing all the tricks of real estate agents will make your home look more luxurious too – draping a cozy throw rug across one arm of the sofa or at the end of your bed, accent pillows on your bed, a cookbook on a display stand in the kitchen, and the book you are currently reading on a side table.

I love to have soft background music playing whenever I am at home and it creates such a nice atmosphere. One day my Aunt came around to drop something off and as she followed me through the house she said, 'It's so serene in here.' And this was just a normal weekday at home with only me there. I was so happy to hear that, because all the things I do for my own sense of deep peace affect others in a positive way as well.

I hope this chapter has been an encouragement that there is so much you can do right now to transform your living space into a glamorous backdrop for your fabulous life, because it's true, there is. Let's go!

Your *Glam Life* tips:

~ Consider that your home is **the centre of everything in your life** and focus on making your home life as good as it can be.

~ **Dream up your 'ideal home style'** list and when you need to replace something, take inspiration as to the style and look, within your budget of course.

~ **Automate what you can** to make home life as easy as possible. Editing your possessions will help. Think clean, tidy, and curated in your own style.

Your *Glam Life* inspirational questions to contemplate:

~ *What does my dream home look like?*

~ *What words describe the feeling of my ideal home?*

~ *How do I want others to feel in my home?*

~ *What are some simple things I can do to bring these descriptions to life?*

~ *What brands do I love that could provide inspiration for my living space?*

~ *What is the easiest category I can curate today?*

~ *What is the most bothersome category that I could edit and it would have a major impact on how I feel in my home?*

~ *What kind of ambience do I want to create?*

Chapter 8.
Inspire dazzling confidence in yourself

Having your own sense of self and the confidence to be you is what makes for a compelling package. Not only to other people, but for yourself as well. As much as we think having confidence will help us navigate social events, the workplace, and other times when we are mixing with people, it also helps us fall in love with *ourselves*. We will be the happiest person around, love our life, and generally have the best fun ever, no matter what the day brings – vacation or working week, fun or chores, rain or shine.

It's easiest to have confidence in yourself when you work on pleasing yourself first, rather than trying to make everyone else happy. For me I know this is when I felt the least secure in myself, when I was doing the latter.

And conversely, even though it felt selfish at the time, when I started working out exactly what I wanted to do in any given situation and actually did it, I not only became happier in myself, but that radiant aura of joy invited others into my orbit. I didn't have to do a thing except bring myself pleasure and follow what gave me joy.

Could it really be possible that we have gotten it around the wrong way for so long? And for some of us most of our life? Looking back it seems to have been that way for me.

I'm still not 'there' yet, but the more I create my own fun, follow the breadcrumbs of what lights me up (in big and small ways), the more my life is turning out to be the most magical fairy tale imaginable.

Walk into a room like you own it

Something I love to do is make an entrance, but in my own unique way. When I think about it, people I admire are not slinking around trying to fade into the background, but neither are they showboating around with a *Look at me!* energy. It's much more subtle than that.

Whether it's running errands or attending an event, I enter the room with a calm sense of *I'm a rockstar*. Because, why not? Why not stand tall with exquisite posture and serene poise? Why not have fun pretending you're a celebrity who has dropped into town for the day?

I have heard different stories about people who *acted as if*, and walked into a venue pretending they were the most beautiful and captivating person ever. And yes, they created their own reality. Heads turned, they received VIP treatment, and had the best night, all from that decision to have a little fun with their state of mind.

Let's consider this as a viewer – we are another person in the room. What we would see is someone with persuasive body language and an empowered energy. We'd see strong posture, a sense of self-assuredness, and a look of *I own the place*. When you see people who are not afraid to take up space in the world you cannot help but be drawn to them, even if there is a tiny aspect of 'Who do they think they are?' But that voice only holds us back. Shall we all just have a stock answer for the next time our inner critic says that to us? I'd suggest, 'I'm Fiona and I'm fabulous' (with your name instead of mine, which would totally make more sense!)

Tony Robbins says that how you hold yourself is how you will feel. So, if you smile, stand tall and project confidence with your physical body, this will also carry through into actual confidence. Combining a mental tune-up with how you feel in your body is an unbeatable combination.

Fake it 'til you make it is true in this situation. You turn up and feel nervous about feeling good enough in front of all the other people there. You give yourself a pep talk, make your entrance, *act as if*, and before you know it you're integrated into the crowd and having a great time. It's a self-fulfilling prophecy.

Focus on your good points

No-one is perfect, even perfect people. I remember hearing model Elle McPherson being interviewed many years ago, and she was asked if there were any parts of her body she didn't like, because it seemed that she had the ideal physique. First, what kind of question is that? How rude! But secondly, she gave a great answer. Elle declined to share, because she said her job as a model was to hide those parts and only show herself in the best light.

I thought that was an excellent response, and it makes sense too. Why on earth would we point out our bad points to anyone else? Is it in case they notice them and we want to get in first? What if instead we decided never to speak about our imperfections and instead focus on what's great about us, in all areas of our life not just our body?

We all have aspects of ourselves that we consider could be better, so let's just park those in the long-term carpark far, far away, and keep close to us all the things we are happy with or can do something about.

We can focus on what we love about our body
We can do our best in the present moment and trust that the future will work itself out, because it always does
We can learn how to manage our money better
We can start preparing meals in a slightly healthier way

There is so much more creativity that leads us towards a sense of relaxed happiness when we focus on all that is good. It really is as simple as that – counting our blessings in whatever area we are currently feeling a little blah about. Don't like what you see? Just look in the other direction!

Reverse the camera

You know when you take a selfie and reverse the camera on your phone? Well, when we walk around thinking about ourselves and how nervous we are walking into a party and hope we can have a 'good conversation' night, or bump into someone we haven't seen in ages and worry about how we look, it's like we spend our whole lives with the reverse camera on.

In the future whenever you have a dip in your confidence, switch your mental camera to focus on what's in front of you rather than your own selfie. Focus on that other person and get to know them, even if you already know them. Ask them questions and let that spark off conversation or further questions.

I always think that everyone else at a party is so confident and at ease, but really, many won't be. A lot of people will be feeling just like you. At a recent work dinner with my husband's company, I was talking to a colleague of his. The man said, 'Where's my wife, she gets a bit lost at these things', and I thought it was really sweet of him to look out for her. I enjoy her company so I stopped for a chat with her too. This brief interaction made me see that most people feel a bit insecure when navigating social situations and small talk. What if we all just relaxed and enjoyed ourselves instead?

I'll have a chance to practice all this again in a few days with another work function coming up. Wish me luck!

Confidence in all areas of your life

Confidence isn't just about social situations either, although for many of us they can be nerve-wracking. There is also feeling confident in your role as a wife/mother/sister/daughter etc. Confidence in your skills in the workplace, the kitchen, and running a household. Confidence with fashion, style and dressing yourself. So many areas!

May I share with you my favourite ways I have found to inspire unshakeable confidence in oneself?

1. **Hold yourself straighter**. Standing tall immediately shifts how you feel, for the better.

2. **Stop any negative thoughts**. You can't know they are really true so just choose to ignore them. Inner mind chatter is not to be trusted for the facts!

3. **Tend to your outer beauty**. It's amazing how good you feel after a shower and dressing in clothes you enjoy, and doing your hair and makeup. Plus finish off with a spritz of fragrance, and fresh nail polish too. You will feel like a million dollars.

4. **Inner work**. Journal a page of happy thoughts, or things that are exciting to you right now. Make a list of projects, plans, dreams, wishes, and things that have gone well; fill a page up and then read back through it. Coming up with a list of everything you have achieved over the past year feels fabulous too, even though it feels a bit vain to do so!

5. **Dive into the positivity lake**. From today onwards vow to keep any negative thoughts to yourself and not give them air. You will speak only of good, fun and uplifting topics. You also won't take in any negative or sensationalist media such as repetitive news stories or rants on social media. Let negativity wither on the vine

and only feed what you want to see more of –
positivity!

6. **Think about your beautiful future** and how
you want it to be. You have to be a bright,
confident and happy person to live that life, so
start to become her now, in this present day.
What you focus on is what you will receive, so
focus on how fabulous *the future you* is.

7. Remind yourself that even though you might
have many flaws, **you are still a precious
jewel** in the grand scheme of life. We are each
the centre of our own universe, so why would we
not claim that birth right? We are worthy of
love, happiness and success every single day of
our existence.

8. **Forget about the past** and how you could
have done some things differently. It's an
impossibility now because that time has gone.
Any memories you have are just stories so
what's the point in holding on to them? The
place where you are right now is *the place*. It's
all you have! Enjoy it! Live every moment!

Your *Glam Life* tips:

~   **Confidence is there for the taking**, it's that simple. Act it then you'll feel it. It's only our self-critical feeling that weighs down heavily on us. Imagine letting that go, and feeling free to be you. Wouldn't that be amazing?

~   Think about **the most confident person you know.** Are they perfect and do they always say or do the right thing? Likely not. But do they let that stop them loving life? No! Try it yourself and see how simple it can be.

Your *Glam Life* inspirational questions to contemplate:

~   *What one simple tip could I employ to feel a greater sense of confidence right now? This very minute? (For me, it's posture. Even sitting down I immediately pull my shoulders back and tuck my tailbone under and it feels so good!)*

~   *Who is the most confident person I know personally and what could I learn from how they are?*

~ *What clothes in my closet make me feel the most confident?*

~ *What other aspects of my personal style could help me feel more poised?*

~ *What beliefs do I wish were true for me? (Confidence is a sense of belief in something. Decide what you'd like your beliefs to be and claim them. Ignore critical comments in your mind and proceed!)*

Chapter 9.
Dress for your dreams

No matter your ideal style, there is always a way to add more zing. You might be happy in general with the style of clothes you wear, but perhaps everything feels a little flat right now and some new *oomph* would really enhance things.

It doesn't necessarily mean spending money either. You can decide in an instant to look the very best with what you've already got – time, money, looks, current wardrobe and makeup collection. What matters is your motivation and what you do with it.

It is so easy to level up your looks when you are inspired to. For me it's watching a television program or movie where everyone has spent time on their makeup, styled their hair, and wear eye-catching outfits. This gives me a spark to play around in my closet and create new outfits, spend a few minutes more on my eye makeup and act as if I am that creative and beautiful creature of glamour whose only job is to look good. And then I carry on with my day!

It's incredible how people will compliment you or even treat you differently when you look better than the average person. I've found that for myself. And mostly I forget that I did something different such as 'light daytime smoky eyes'. It's not until someone says, 'Where are you going all dressed up?' or 'Your eyes look gorgeous like that' and I remember, *Oh, yes, I have bombshell eyes today.*

As described in Day 4 of my book *Thirty Chic Days: Practical inspiration for a beautiful life*, it's fun to practice your eye makeup daily if you can. Not only do you look great, but you get better at it the more you do it.

Blend *your* style with glamour

Glamour is not just one type. Most of us will have an image of glamour that is old Hollywood: red lipstick, tumbling glossy brunette wavy hair and oversized black sunglasses. But you can infuse glamour into any type of personal style and volumize it to be *next-level*. Imagine casual glamour, sporty glamour or boho glamour.

Whatever your favourite style cue is, you can add glamour to it and elevate it. I would describe my personal style as casual, classic, 5% boho, French

Chic. How I have been glamourizing my style is by:

~ **Adding more colour**. For a while now I have felt drawn to brighter, clearer shades whereas before that I was a neutrals and soft 'faded' palette girl. The only brights in my closet were slightly more saturated pastels. Now my most favourite items are a red boho eyelet blouse and a sunny yellow linen top with balloon sleeves. These pieces make me feel so happy when I wear them. I'm not trying to analyse just why I am so attracted to colour now, I'm just enjoying it!

~ **Adding more gold**. Gold touches always look so luxe to me. Gold paired with *anything* makes it look better. So, I'll choose a bag or belt with gold hardware not silver. I'll wear my gold (costume or real) jewellery more. And I wear warm-toned shades more than cool tones in makeup too.

~ **Wearing a cocktail ring**. My cocktail ring is not a giant semi-precious stone (but I would love one like that – maybe smoky quartz or citrine). I have a couple that are made from pretty shades of resin, and I wear one on my right hand. It really adds a dimension of fun and colour. There are so many beautiful rings, both fine jewellery and costume, and you feel so different when you wear a cocktail ring – far more glamorous!

~ **Going 'next-level' with my makeup application**. Working from home, sometimes the only person I see in a day is my husband. If I had a busy home day where I wasn't going out, sometimes I wouldn't put any makeup on at all. I thought it saved me time, but realistically it only takes me about ten minutes to put on quick makeup. And I enjoy doing it too. It feels artistic and creative, and I love to receive value from the items I have purchased in the past. So, I have upgraded home days to *quick makeup*, and days when I want to go out to *bombshell makeup*. Bombshell makeup to me is still quite light; it's not Instagram makeup but it's more than I would usually wear. I see how good it looks and this makes me happy to do it. And it's actually very relaxing. I play an inspiring listenable YouTube video while I decorate my 'canvas' and it's a meditative way to begin my day.

These are just a few of the ways in which I have been intentionally adding more glamour to my personal style. Maybe some of them appeal to you, or perhaps ask yourself, *How can I do a little bit more with what I've got?*

The quickest way to upgrade your look

Mostly I wear flats during the day, but sometimes, just for fun I'll wear the exact same outfit with heels. No, they're not as comfortable as flats, but they're not uncomfortable either, if you know what I mean. And for a couple of hours I can feel more glamorous – even a mid-height heel feels more elevated (quite literally!)

You will probably already have shoes in your closet that you deem 'only for special occasions' or 'slightly *too much* for everyday wear' (whatever that means). But why not get your money's worth from them. You don't need to go shopping to pump up your look when you utilize your current wardrobe.

It's quite incredible how the same outfit can look completely different with another pair of shoes. Try it for yourself.

And if any of your shoes give off frumpy vibes, put them in your donation box! Life is too short to feel older than you are. I know it's a fine line between dressing too young and aging yourself, but I think you know deep down when something is not doing you any favours.

And when you do go shopping for shoes, consider more colourful and fun options. Steer clear of sensible and practical. Buy the red pair instead of the black. Choose leopard print. I promise you they will still go with everything! Very few pairs of shoes I have now are not coloured or patterned, and the few black pairs I have are rarely worn.

Even if you haven't worked your way up to actually buying them, go and have a try on of some and see how good they make you look and feel. You might be surprised that they aren't so far out of your comfort zones – both physical and mental.

Find your fashion mentors

You will likely have a few people in mind who are your style icons, whether you know them in real life or from online, in magazines or while watching a movie. Choose the one who is top of mind right now and fashion your style after theirs. All you need to do is add a few components that they have into *your* look – maybe it's a silky head scarf, long earrings, or a bright lipstick.

Two I have at the moment are:

Riviera: This series is set on the Côte d'Azur, and as well as the houses being fabulous, the main female characters played by Lena Olin and Julia Stiles are très chic. They wear colourful flowing maxi-dresses, wide-leg pants with camisoles and nipped-waist jackets and other outfits that are both beautiful and glamorous. Watching this series has inspired me to add more colour into my wardrobe as well as experiment with different clothing silhouettes than I usually wear. I want some of that easy warm-weather glamour!

Selling Sunset: The ladies on this series are all driven, highly polished real estate agents, and I love to see their off-duty outfits too. They are all far more 'extra' than my own personal style, but they have encouraged me to dress up more and not be so casual all the time. There is plenty of room for improvement in my daily dress without being inappropriately over-the-top.

Consider your favourite book, movie, fashion magazine or someone whose personal style you admire currently and make notes for your own use. It's so fun to add in a few energizing tidbits to elevate your dress.

Elegant at home

What you wear at home is just as important as what you wear when you go out. It is beneficial for your self-identity to be congruent in all areas of your life as much as possible – it is certainly a luxurious goal to aim for, don't you think? Being the elegant lady in all areas of your life?

Dressing well at home, in a manner that suits you, your lifestyle and your budget is just one way you can elevate your outlook. If I don't have anything to go to on a normal day, I will dress in an outfit that is comfortable and practical, but that is also polished and makes me feel happy.

And before dinner, even though I work from home now and no longer go to an office, I like to change into loungewear. When you change clothes your mind instantly switches gears, from productive efficiency to *Aah, I can relax now*. It's a wonderful feeling. I am all about having a helpful mindset, but there are also many external changes you can make that will help you achieve the mental state you desire

– in this case – serenity and peace of mind.

For my loungewear, I like to dress in *luxurious comfort*. Doesn't that sound delicious? Colourful or printed satin pieces are the perfect embodiment of that phrase to me, and in the cooler months snuggly cashmere-like pieces fit the bill. I say 'cashmere-like' because I don't like to spend too much money on my home loungewear. Everything is washed often and I cook dinner in it, so I'd cry if I ruined actual cashmere.

Luckily you will find plentiful options if you look around, at prices that are budget friendly. If you sew, you can even make your own satin pieces – think palazzo pants, floaty shorts, camisole tops and kimono style jackets or longer toppers.

There really isn't a single area of your personal style that can't be made more glamorous, and it's such a fun project too. Loungewear, nightwear, exercise clothes – nothing is off limits!

Your *Glam Life* tips:

~ **Dress well but don't obsess**. Do the work beforehand and enjoy the process of getting dressed and made up, but then forget all about it, instead focusing on who you are with or what you are doing.

~ **Tidy your closet and keep it that way**. Having an organized closet makes it far easier to curate a glamorous personal style. It is just more relaxing to get dressed and look good every day when you plan your wardrobe and be intentional with it.

~ **Edit your wardrobe with numbers**. I heard advice to remove one-third and it really appealed! Even if just for a trial. Count the garments in that category and choose your favourites until you get to two-thirds, then the rest go on probation, or preferably into a donation box or the bin depending on their condition.

~ **Upgrade your shoe choices**. Shoes are an easy way to change your look. Consider swapping out your usual flat sandals for a pair of platform wedges. When you go to buy a new pair of winter ankle books, how about a one-inch heel instead of flats? It doesn't always have to be about the heel height, but even a little bit of an elevation changes everything. If you can only wear flats, try a different colour, or even a print such as leopard.

~ Consider **how intentional you are with the clothes you wear at home**. If you are like me and prefer to change for the evening, are you still projecting the image you wish to portray about your ideal self? Or are you letting yourself down with old, frumpy, or worn-out clothes just because they are functional and comfortable? It doesn't need to cost much to upgrade your home loungewear, or you may already have items you can repurpose.

Your *Glam Life* inspirational questions to contemplate:

~ *Who are my favourite style icons right now? What about them appeals, and can I add some of their ideas and flavours into my personal style?*

~ *What are my current favourite clothing and accessory items, and why am I drawn to them so much? (Wear those items more and keep them in mind when you need to go shopping.)*

~ *Brainstorm twenty ways in which you can infuse glamour into your look right now, with what you already have. Is it changing the combinations in which you wear clothes? More colour? Less colour? Different makeup? More time spent doing your hair or wearing it loose rather than in a ponytail?*

Chapter 10.

Create an at-home vacation-every-day feeling

The word 'vacation' means to get away from or escape ('vacate' is at the beginning of the word). But why not create a beautiful life experience that you get to enjoy every day rather than just for a few weeks once a year – and that's if you're lucky!

When we moved to a different part of the country four years ago and were looking at a house to buy, I specifically wanted to create an 'on holiday' lifestyle where it felt like we were on vacation every day. It doesn't mean I wanted to sit around doing nothing but read a book all the time, but I did desire to meld both my daily life with vacation life for a relaxed, fun and easy feeling.

I feel like I have achieved that now, so let's go

through what I did over time to get that delightfully relaxed feeling of vacation life.

Firstly, I brainstormed all the elements of being on holiday that I loved, things such as:

~ Having a small, curated wardrobe appropriate for that area and season, with only my nicest and most favourite items of clothing.
~ Going out to eat, or having food in our room such as fresh tropical fruit for breakfast.
~ Meandering around experiencing a new place.
~ Dressing up for a day of sightseeing.
~ No housework, chores or laundry to do.
~ No jobs or errands hanging over me.
~ No to-do list.
~ Nothing to do except relax and recuperate.
~ Going shopping and buying a few new fun things such as clothing or cosmetics.
~ The freedom to rest at any time of the day.
~ Being outside feeling the sun on my skin.
~ A cocktail at happy hour before heading out for dinner.
~ Lying on a sun lounger by the pool.
~ Having the time to do my hair and makeup in a relaxed manner each morning.
~ Effortless exercise due to sightseeing.
~ Excited to come back home with all my new inspiration afterwards.

After that, it was fun to see how I could integrate as many of these things as possible into my everyday life. And it also made previously dull tasks such as decluttering, organizing my closet, and tidying our home easier, because I had the mindset of 'vacation lifestyle'.

A spacious, easy place to live

It's amazing how much we pack into our homes 'just in case', but when we're on holiday we seem to get by with just what's in our bag. Not only did this thought assist me in filling my donation box with items we never seemed to get around to using, but it also helped curb unnecessary spending.

This was good for our bank account, and also for the storage spaces in our home. I started looking around to see how I could make an area look roomier and more appealing, just like in a hotel room or a vacation rental. Even people who have a second holiday home seem to keep far less there than at their primary residence.

Dressing well every day

When going on vacation, I take a bag with my favourite clothes and only the makeup I'll actually use. Translating this to my everyday life means creating a seasonal wardrobe of my nicest things that are appropriate for how I spend my day, and doing the same with cosmetics.

When it comes to makeup, this helps me overcome the desire to buy more, because I know I have plenty at home, and it's rarely about getting a different colour, it's just about having something new.

No chores in a vacation lifestyle

I try to minimize tasks in my daily life as much as possible. Less items in my home means less to clean, organize, pay for, store, and insure. I have outsourced some tasks such as having a cleaner come in once a week.

I debated this for a long time, but finally justified it to myself by looking at the things I don't spend money on that others do. I only buy a coffee maybe once or twice a month and it's only because I am meeting someone 'for coffee'. I know people who buy a coffee every day and sometimes twice a day. I eat most of my meals at home, which is also a huge saving. These things more than pay for my cleaner, whom I adore. Plus, I am helping out another family with her employment.

I stay on top of laundry and this helps keep things feeling easy because there is never a big pile. We don't try to wait 'just one more meal' to run our dishwasher so that it's not a huge chore to unload. If I plant something new in the garden it is easy-care because I am not a person who enjoys pottering around outside for leisure.

Simplifying my life means that my to-do list has

disappeared. I have a planner where I write tasks or reminders on certain days so I remember them, but there is no burdensome list hanging over me. I've simply let some things fall away and my life has not become worse because of this, but instead better. Sometimes we keep doing things simply because we have always done them. Question everything!

Time to yourself on holiday

I purposely don't add tons of activities into my day because I value time to myself. In the past when I have signed up for group classes I have instantly regretted it. I know myself well enough now that I don't like that trapped feeling of having a busy schedule, or even of having to be somewhere at a certain time each week. Some thrive on it but not me. I don't feel bad anymore and really, no-one probably cares anyway; they're too busy worrying about themselves and their own schedule.

Then, because our life is not all planned and booked out in advance, we can be spontaneous on the weekend and go out to a winery for lunch or do something touristy. We can wander around our own city and join visitors to the region as they enjoy strolling the streets looking at what is unique to this area.

Cocktail hour

We have an outdoor terrace at our place, but in an effort to make it more resort-like, I now tend the flowering pots more frequently and sweep up regularly. Because we do it often, it only takes five minutes, and we then get to sit outside in the summer and enjoy a cold drink.

I'd love to buy a pair of sun loungers and have them be available to us too. Nothing says 'relax and enjoy yourself' like having your feet elevated and a book by your side. And really, what difference does it make if I spend half an hour browsing the internet, or reading a book outside? Both are free time, but one feels like I'm on holiday and the other... doesn't.

In the winter our cocktail hour involves lighting the wood burner and putting music on. Aspen vibes perhaps? We'll play a YouTube walking tour on television with the sound muted, or something fun such as a Chanel fashion show or a luxury hotel review to be glamorous moving wallpaper while we chat.

Simplified food supplies

I don't know about you, but on vacation our hotel room does *not* contain a fridge full of half-used condiments, pantry items spilling out everywhere and a freezer packed with mystery items. No, either we will be eating out, or we will have a few items in our fridge such as a container of tropical fruit purchased for breakfast the next morning, to have with yoghurt and chopped nuts.

Carrying this through to my home life, I started intentionally using up all the items I'd bought and then didn't know what to do with. If I really didn't want to use them or they had expired, I gave myself permission to throw them out without guilt. This was difficult for me because I don't like to waste money, and I also feel bad that I have wasted food. But I wasted it by not using it in the first place, not by throwing it out. On a few occasions when I have included something borderline subpar in a meal just to use it up, it felt like I was eating that product just to get rid of it – in effect treating my body like a garbage bin!

Nowadays I get such a thrill from having an almost-empty, bright, clean fridge that I get to fill up with colourful produce, buying only the items I know I will use within the next week. Having to throw things out which means quite literally throwing money in the bin has made me much stricter at the supermarket. I ask myself honestly if I will ever use this item that I am contemplating buying. Sometimes the answer is no.

Our pantry and freezer are the same. I had a period of time where I purposely did not buy anything except what we actually needed and got my supplies down. I did what all the home economics people say to do by checking what I had at home and supplementing those items with purchased groceries to make meals. It is rudimentary but I had ignored this advice for a while. It feels far more relaxing to have a kitchen that is not overwhelmed with loads of ingredients that don't even actually go together!

Start where you are

All of these changes didn't happen overnight. I've been perfecting my at-home vacation lifestyle for a number of years now, and I definitely still fall down sometimes. I'll overstock on something and then remember, *Oh yes, I don't like that crowded feeling, it doesn't feel good to me.* Maybe that's not a bad thing – it is a chance to remember the feeling I desire.

You will find though, as you slowly start integrating small changes into your daily life, that you will have little pockets of time open up in which you can rest and recuperate. You will feel like you have a chance to relax and rejuvenate just like when you're on holiday.

That way, your actual vacation time will be like a wonderful cherry on the top of your at-home holiday lifestyle.

Your *Glam Life* tips:

~ Let this chapter sink in and know that yes, a permanent **on-vacation feeling is available to you** year-round, even if you work full-time, even if you have a young family. It will look different for everyone, for sure, but you can certainly tweak things if you want to.

~ Brainstorm your own list of favourite past holiday activities, feelings, and ways to relax, or how you might **imagine an ideal vacation** in the future. Include as many little details as you can.

~ Choose a category and **add in something small** (or subtract something perhaps). A simple purchase I made was a ceramic Starbucks mug for my home coffee (I usually only ever have Starbucks on vacation so it gives me a happy, excited feeling).

~ Carry that **relaxed vacation mindset** around with you as much as possible. For me this is probably the most important thing. Let your mind slow down, don't worry about all the things that haven't happened yet. Simply let your thoughts pass without judgement and know that everything will be fine. You're on holiday!

Your *Glam Life* inspirational questions to contemplate:

~ *Where have my favourite vacations been in the past?*

~ *What have I liked about them?*

~ *What kinds of things did we do that I particularly enjoyed?*

~ *How many of those things can I include in my daily life here where I live?*

~ *What kinds of feelings make me feel like I'm on holiday and how can I intentionally cultivate them for myself?*

Chapter 11.

Cultivate beauty rituals

In your glamorously new upleveled life, why not decide to be *the glam goddess*? The star in your own movie? In this chapter I am bringing the vibe of old Hollywood – why not channel it for yourself?

Think of Marilyn Monroe, Greta Garbo, or Katharine Hepburn... can you see them in your mind pampering themselves in their beautiful bedroom? Wrapped in a flowing silky robe, sitting at their dressing table massaging cold cream into their face to cleanse their skin before bedtime?

Deciding to be the kind of lady who regularly performs her own beauty rituals has a two-fold effect. Firstly, you are looking after your skin and ensuring that your complexion looks as good as it can for as long as it can. And secondly, you are pampering yourself at the same time.

We all have different aspects of beauty that we enjoy doing more than others. I love caring for my skin, putting on and taking off makeup, and doing my nails. I don't enjoy doing my hair so much. It takes so long to wash in the shower, and forever to dry. I also am not very good at blow-drying it so it never sits quite right!

With the things I enjoy, I revel in them and thoroughly enjoy the time it takes to do them. And with the hair styling, I love the feel and look of clean, bouncy hair, so I do my best. I 'just do it' and I also do it as quickly as I can, otherwise I will procrastinate all day. And, my goal is to change my mindset around it. Some reframing of thoughts plus a few YouTube tutorials is my plan.

The common theme whether you particularly enjoy something or not is to have rituals for yourself and put energy into them.

And there's nothing to say that you have to do everything either. For many years I didn't paint my nails, I just kept them neat and clean with my cuticles pushed back and plenty of hand lotion and nail cream. But currently I love having shiny polished nails.

Glamour = impeccable hygiene

You need to care for your body every day, so why not make it a fun, enjoyable and beautiful experience for yourself? You know how you feel after a long shower when you have exfoliated all over and washed and conditioned your hair? It's a priceless sensation that makes feeling glamorous a given.

I am a shower girl, and my shower contains a small selection of products that I enjoy using. I have a back loofah, and a pumice stone for my feet. I even have a small inexpensive Bluetooth speaker to listen to an audiobook if I want to.

At night I like to put on my Dior Relaxing Music playlist from Spotify and wash my face in a peaceful environment. My husband is still watching television down the hall, so our bedroom and ensuite is the scene for my spa time before bed. Even brushing and flossing my teeth feels relaxing when I am in peaceful boudoir time mode.

Curate items you enjoy using and care for your skin with intention. My favourite skincare products have natural fragrances such as lavender and other essential oils.

Your rich lady life

There are two types of beauty rituals:

Things you have to do anyway
Things you'd love to do in your idealistic dream life

I wrote mine down in each of these two categories and thought I'd share them to start you thinking about yours:

Daily tasks

~ Brushing and flossing my teeth (twice daily brush, once daily floss)
~ Washing and moisturizing my face at night
~ A shower in the morning and full body moisturization
~ Washing my hair (2-3 times per week)
~ Using a pumice stone on my feet (twice a week)
~ Shaving or epilating my legs (1-3 times per week)
~ Putting makeup and fragrance on each day
~ Filing and painting my nails (once a week)
~ Massaging cream into my décolletage, hands, and feet before bed

Beauty rituals in my idealistic rich lady life

~ A proper blow-dry doing my hair in layers with a big round brush
~ Applying glowy shimmer or self-tan
~ Tinting my eyebrows every 3-4 weeks
~ Exfoliating my body in the shower
~ Running a bath in the winter and soaking with Epsom salts, essential oils, and a book.

If there is anything you wish you did but never do, write it on your idealistic rich lady list and choose one to do this week. From this list, I have been applying self-tanner to my arms, legs, and décolletage, even though we are going into winter here. No-one outside the house will see my legs, but it feels good to be tanned. And if I am suddenly invited away on a tropical trip, I will be prepared! After all, when you live the *Glam Life,* anything can happen!

Your hygiene rituals are required every day anyway, so why not make them nicer, more luxurious. And then add healthy and fun rituals into your day as well. For a relatively small time investment and very little if any monetary cost, you will feel like the wealthiest, most pampered lady ever.

The ultimate in self-care

Not only does performing your beauty tasks have a payoff in how you look, but there is a wonderful side benefit – *it is so relaxing.* If you have ever had a spa treatment, you will recall that the tranquil and pampering atmosphere is part of the experience.

When you create your own spa rituals at home you will feel indulged, time will slow down, and you will feel calmer. When you enjoy what you are doing every day, life becomes better.

And the more energy you put into your own self-care, the more energy you have to give to others. When you pamper and take care of yourself, and look your best, you feel happier and that good feeling spreads. Simply put, when you take time for yourself, you are a nicer person to those around you. Everyone benefits.

Your *Glam Life* tips:

~ Choose to see yourself as someone who partakes in the **feminine mystery of daily beauty rituals**; take on that identity for yourself.

~ Brainstorm a list of rituals you currently do, and ponder how you can make them feel **more luxurious** and relaxed, plus start a wish list of experiences you would enjoy.

~ Be **intentional and present** when you are doing something as simple as brushing and flossing your teeth. Be there with yourself, experience the lovely clean feeling.

~ Let yourself **feel calm and pampered** – daily.

Your *Glam Life* inspirational questions to contemplate:

~ *What would the glamorous movie star me do for self-care and beauty on a regular basis?*

~ *What would it take for me to be able to include more beauty rituals in my life as it is right now?*

~ *What is the payoff if I let myself be pampered more?*

Chapter 12.

Perform your own glow-up

You may have heard the term *glow-up* that has been going around lately. Don't you love the sound of a glow-up? It's just so enticing. If you haven't heard this term, it's like a good old-fashioned makeover or even a comeback, but goes further than that. You can choose to have a glow-up in any area of your life, and focus on improving both your inner beauty as well as your outer beauty.

It's quite a thrilling thing to consider, especially when you come at it from a content place; you get to enhance what you are already happy with. You can love yourself exactly as you are, *and* it is exciting to see how much further you can go. There is no limit to how good things can become!

The Collins dictionary says of someone who 'glows up', that they become more mature, confident, and attractive. Another great online definition said, "become the best version of yourself, find interests, improve your style, strengthen your mindset, and build an overall foundation for the type of person you aspire to grow into". There is so much inspiring goodness in that sentence alone.

It is fun to think about all the different categories of your life that could benefit from a glow-up, and then choose one or two to start with. The possibilities are limitless – honestly, you will feel like a child in a candy store.

Here is a delicious-looking menu for you to peruse, and order from:

Developing **inner beauty** of kindness, gentleness, and charity.

Improving your mental state by focusing on serenity, peace of mind, inner calm, and self-development.

Having a **health glow-up** with a consistent sleeping regime, more natural/less processed food, and drinking more water.

A **beauty glow-up**: Looking after your skin, moisturizing more, trying new makeup styles, learning how to best handle your hair type, playing up your eyes with more mascara, feeling confident in your own skin and expressing your creativity when you make up your face.

A **fashion and style glow-up**: Finding out what clothing suits your body type and what colours suit your colouring best.

Make it a party

Like anything worthwhile, a glow-up requires focus and effort, but that doesn't mean you can't have a good time doing it. In fact, I believe fun and enjoyment are key factors in my own success in any area. If you have read any of my other books you will have picked up on this. If something is dull, boring, worthy-without-reward, or any other combination of uninspiring words, I just can't make myself do it. And you may be the same.

Your betterment journey can be as dry and dreary or as juicy and sparkling as you want, so why not choose to have a 'glamorous glow-up' over, say, a 'three-part self-improvement routine' or whatever other lacklustre corporate-style language description you can think of.

Sell it to yourself like a savvy marketer. Take all the things you'd love to upgrade in your life and rephrase them to sound like the most exciting and interesting choices ever. Be your own target audience! List all the benefits of a glow-up in case your initial enthusiasm fades. Then, you can remember those along with your enticing outcome.

With a Glamorous Glow-Up you will:

~   Grow your confidence, creativity, and self-discipline.
~   Learn new things about yourself.
~   Maybe find a new side hustle.
~   Make daily life more enjoyable.
~   Find a new lease on life.
~   See what you are capable of.

When you choose just one thread to pull on or one breadcrumb to follow, you'll find paths open up to you in directions you'd never even dreamed of. Miracles will occur!

The wonder of inner beauty

I have been a journaller and practitioner of inner work for more than three decades, and I still have a long way to go because the study never ends. You get to go deeper and further, and also learn that *embodying* what you have learned is key.

As you do your self-study work, you will become happier, more at peace, more effortlessly productive, and *more of who you are*. You get to see that who you are is okay, more than okay. You own everything about yourself at the same time as striving for more.

And as you do this, you see that everyone else is the same. They are doing the best with the knowledge they have. When you realize this, you become softer, more accepting, more forgiving. You reduce your expectations from others down to zero, and take them as they are. You experience them in a different way as well as strengthening your own boundaries.

Aren't these all beautiful things to receive?

Have fun with your outer beauty

And then there is the fun of levelling up your look. Just like a makeover on the *Oprah* show back in the day, you get to paint an inspiring vision for yourself and go for it. In no particular order, here is my glow-up wishlist that I've been working on, one or two categories at a time.

~ Perfecting my hair game – learning how to blow-dry and style my hair like a professional
~ Being creative with my eye makeup
~ Tidying my closet and trying new outfit combinations
~ Decluttering clothes that aren't the next-level me and keeping only the clothes that make me ring with happiness
~ Upleveling my personal style to be more sophisticated and colourful
~ Having a nicely done manicure at all times
~ Using cuticle oil often
~ Having smooth legs with self-tan
~ Improving my posture

~ Going for a brisk walk every day
~ Stretching often throughout the day

It's fun to have a floating theme and pick and choose like in a candy store, and sometimes you might decide on one point and really go for it.

I took the focused approach with some pandemic/menopause weight gain almost a year ago. I lost five kilos (about eleven pounds) and have kept it off, which I am thrilled with. I believe I was successful because:

~ I upgraded to a 'No matter what' mindset.
~ I journaled about it every day.
~ I wrote down my successful 'after story'.
~ I listed powerful affirmations of how I desired to be.
~ I noted down how I could make it fun and easy for myself.
~ I crafted new beliefs on how I could go forward in a slim and healthy body as a fifty-plus year old.

No matter how you style your glow-up and what you decide to start with, make sure you approach any desired change from the angle of fun and excitement. No dreading or 'shoulding' is allowed and this way you will find success far easier to come by.

Your *Glam Life* tips:

~ **Be inspired to do your own glow-up**. Research 'glow-up' or 'level-up' and note down as many categories as you can, then choose one or two to start with. Or you might have one major glow-up idea that you know will kickstart everything else, such as slimming down. You might focus on weight loss, or perhaps a connection that you know will help, such as decluttering and organizing your kitchen or closet in an inspiring way.

~ Combine equal amounts of **inner and outer beauty** to maintain harmony and balance.

~ **Enjoy the process**. You are doing it to better yourself and your life, so take it easy, give yourself grace, and find joy in the daily doing. Dream about the outcome and inspire yourself with all the little steps it will take to get there, then forget about it and just focus on the process, with ease and play of course!

Your *Glam Life* inspirational questions to contemplate:

~   *What are all the little things I could do for my own glow-up?*

~   *What do I wish I was better at doing?*

~   *How could I increase my sense of inner peace and happiness?*

~   *What would be a dream outcome from my glow-up?*

Chapter 13.
Be the elegant lady

Choosing to live your life from a place of elegance is more than just how you dress or sip your tea. It is cultivating a sense of calm, being unhurried and unbothered. It is being languid in your movements – slowing them down and making them graceful and fluid.

You can do all of these things in a natural and subtle way and it's amazing how people change around you. They become more attentive, and more respectful. When you are out, or even at home, think 'languid' to yourself and notice how you start to saunter, walking from the hips. You will no longer be charging along like a sergeant major!

I shared in one of my other books that a guy who had taken me out on a date once asked, 'Why do you walk like a man?' Of course he was very rude to say this – I was mortified! – but it was actually a real gift because I never realized that people could 'see' me stomping around.

Maybe you too? I get it, we all have lots on our plate and it seems the only way to get through our never-ending to-do list is to be in our masculine all the time, forgetting that our natural state is as a feminine being. So let's try something different; let's choose instead to *saunter*.

And amazingly, on days when I intentionally decide to move slower and not rush, I actually get more done. Plus I have a nicer day. Additionally, when I dress for my day and do my hair and makeup, I am also more productive. You'd think activewear and a messy bun would be the recipe for efficiency, but I have found the opposite!

Enjoy all eyes on you as you make your life your runway. Your life can feel glamorous as well as getting everything done. And remember to wear fragrance while you do it – smelling good is a virtue, as is looking good for yourself and others!

Being present in your life

A simple change that has helped me increase my elegance quotient is to live in the moment and be more present to those around me. It's an ongoing focus, but a huge part of it is getting off my devices – both when I am with someone and if I am by myself.

When I am sitting at a table, my phone is in my bag, or somewhere else if we're at home. If I do want to look something up, I'll do that and then put my phone away again. It is *so* easy to 'just check a few emails' and then read something else and something else. It's impolite to the person sitting next to you!

You will also find you are more able to be present *for yourself* if you read from a paper book or Kindle. You will not be distracted by notifications on your phone. It's amazing how many times I have picked up my phone to look at something specific and then had my attention diverted away from the task by something else that pops up. I then completely forget about what I wanted to look up because my attention has been hijacked!

And aside from devices, I have endeavoured to listen better, be there fully, and to sit in the moment. Not dreaming of days gone by or being concerned about the future. It's a gift you can give yourself too.

And enunciating words! I am a notoriously soft speaker, and I talk quickly. This is a recipe for people having to ask me to repeat what I said and it's tiresome for everyone. My brain works so quickly that I often tumble my words out – does this sound elegant to you? I'd love to talk slower, think before I speak, and articulate clearly. I have noticed that people I admire never seem rushed, and are easily able to say what they mean. Point taken, and a fun challenge too!

And when it comes to online, you would be wise to enjoy online content in appropriate amounts, otherwise you are not living your own life, you are living someone else's. Isn't this a sobering thought? I know when I spend too much time browsing online, even though it's fun at the time, I feel yucky afterwards; antsy, unsatisfied, and grumpy. It's because I haven't been producing anything myself such as writing, cooking, sewing, or participating in my own real life.

Hours can be taken from us each day unless we are intentional about our online time. Sometimes I will say to myself that the only time I will spend on my computer today is to write my books and/or a social media post, as well as returning friends emails.

But I get it, the lines are blurred these days more than ever. Many of us work online. We order necessities such as groceries online. And we relax online, but is it really a good way to spend our downtime as well? With so much of our time spent in front of a screen, it's beneficial to step away.

When you are starting to feel like you've been plugged in too much, it feels lovely to step outside into nature and be around realness. You will be more present in your life, more present for yourself, and more present for your loved ones. You will be enchanting!

Even leaving your phone in a separate room makes a big difference, otherwise you are always checking it. When I leave my phone charging in the kitchen and my iPad is stored away, I know I am more present with my husband after dinner.

This is something 'new' we are having to deal with as a human species. Computers and especially other devices are designed to capture our attention. It feels far more elegant and just *peaceful* to keep them in their rightful place. It feels far better to remember that *we* are in charge of our own mind, not other people or companies via our phone.

A delightfully feminine being

Becoming the elegant lady is so much easier when you reside in *a feminine state of mind*. Keep this as your filter and you will find yourself effortlessly being more elegant. Infuse a feminine essence in everything you do. Let yourself soften and relax, and almost lean back within your physical body.

Being feminine is said to be strong on the inside and soft on the outside, so it's not about letting people walk all over you. Rather, you have assured preferences in how you want to be, and you let people know in a natural and gentle way by how you are, rather than having to tell them.

When you surround yourself with femininity it is easier to be elegant in your mind. Details that will help you remain feminine are:

~ Making sure you have had enough rest.
~ Quality food (including protein and not too many carbs to keep you feeling on an even keel mood-wise).

~   Keep your nervous system calm by working methodically through your tasks.

~   Playing soft relaxing background music.

~   Not expecting yourself to work like a pack-horse.

You can get the same jobs done in the same amount of time with completely different energy. Many of us reside in an unhelpful stressed feeling simply from habit. It can be difficult to change your feeling state but it's not impossible, and once I saw how good it felt to go through my day in a gentle feminine flow, it was hard to go back to masculine hustle.

This is how you can cultivate an elegant state of mind, and it feels genuine too: your inside matches your desired outside. You will have a radiance about you that others can't put their finger on.

It's so fun to see just how you can upgrade your elegance in all areas of your life, so make your everyday joyful and glamorous – be the elegant lady with your queenly presence.

Your *Glam Life* tips:

~   Decide that from today onwards **you are going to be the elegant lady of your life**. Feel the luxury of that thought as you do your usual things.

~ Think back to times when you are most likely to consume mindless internet content and **see if there are other ways you can relax**. I replaced online scrolling with a juicy Penny Vincenzi novel that's as thick as a doorstop. It feels like a far more luxurious and 'lady of leisure' way to spend my downtime.

Your *Glam Life* inspirational questions to contemplate:

~ *How can I add an aura of elegance to my everyday tasks?*

~ *How can I behave more elegantly?*

~ *Do I feel elegant on the inside? How can I change that?*

~ *How can I slow down my internal pace so that elegance comes more naturally?*

~ *How would I rather spend time if I'm not always on the computer?*

~ *What are some fun and/or useful tasks that I 'never seem to have time for' that I could incorporate into my routine if I cut back on screen time?*

Chapter 14.

Live by your values

Living in alignment with what is important to us is the foundation of a well-lived life. When you are sure of who you are on the inside, it radiates out and you become magnetic to others. When you are a genuine person who loves life and there are no hidden motives, people respond to that: they know you're the real deal.

Knowing what you value and having a quiet confidence in your worth shows in the way you carry yourself. You can be that glamorous woman who has chosen to live the life of her dreams and be happy no matter what. When you carry this surety around you will be fascinating, magical, charming, and all things beautiful. You become a beguiling package!

So, what do you value? When I asked this question of myself, I got that I value peace, contentment, financial security, a quiet life, and health. I value freedom too: the ability to do what I want to do and not be bossed around. And I also love the pretty things such as dressing well, looking good, and having a nicely decorated home that makes me happy to be there. This translates to beauty, elegance and sophistication. I have built these values into my life over the years and made choices based on them.

If you get stuck for ideas, search for 'values list' or 'list of values' online and you'll get some great resources to inspire your list. Another excellent way to find out what you value is to look at what you spend money on.

And then comes the fun part: are you living in alignment with the words that came to you? It can be confronting when you see very plainly, that no, I am not currently living a peaceful, content, simple and free life (or whatever words are important to you).

But the great thing is now you have a direction to aim for, and as you consider all the different areas of your life you can run them through your values filter.

You get to choose

This book is all about living the glam life, of enhancing your life as it is right now, with the fabulous filter of G L A M. So how do we do this? How do we intertwine our love for say, simple living and cozy minimalism, with a feeling of glamour?

When I think about being a glamorous person, they would be someone who lives an exciting life, dresses elegantly, and has grace and poise on every occasion. I am not a person who attends fancy galas or goes out on her yacht, but I can still be that glamorous lady in my own simple, content and peaceful life, *and* have grace and poise too. We can all elevate where we currently are with a sprinkling of who we desire to be.

That's the fun part, when we ask our higher self questions such as: *How can I combine glamour with simplicity? How can I be a glamorous minimalist? Or, How can I live a simple life in a glamorous way?*

Most importantly a glamorous person is someone who has a kind heart, and that's the key. It's all very well looking good on the outside, but if your heart is made of stone it will shine through to the world! I know you are not like that. You are a gentle, kind, loving person. You do your best for others at the same time as having firm boundaries around yourself.

When you are glamorous you possess grace and beauty. You have an appealing sparkle which makes you special. You naturally enchant and delight people. Your inner light makes you attractive and alluring: no matter what you wear, you magically stand out. You have confidence and maturity which comes from knowing who you are and being comfortable with yourself.

Age is no barrier either. Some of the most glamorous ladies I know are much older than me. They have charm, style and elegance in everything they do and it's so inspiring to know that *we can only get better* as we get older. Isn't that wonderful?

Put together your *Who I Am* list

I created this for myself a while back and have also written about the concept in my book *Loving Your Epic Small Life* (*Chapter 17. Making peace with a bad situation*). My *Who I Am* list is still going strong and continues to inspire me to be my best.

You can create your own version by starting with attributes you admire in others – note them all down. Then think about qualities you particularly dislike, and *write the opposite*. An example from mine is that I don't want to be one of those people always on their phones, so I wrote 'participates in real life', 'reads paper books', 'has hobbies and interests', 'makes things', 'educated' and 'aware' as opposites.

An online thesaurus (I use thesaurus.com) is great for finding similar words to add to your list, and also antonyms for attributes you don't like.

It took me a while to put my list together, it definitely wasn't a five-minute job. And of course you can add to it over time. After I had compiled a big, beautiful list of words, I grouped them into like categories for clarity. Here is my *Who I Am* list and I hope you are inspired to create your own!

Clean   *Tidy*
Orderly   *Kempt*
Organized

Active
Energetic
Fresh
Interested
Lively
Vivacious
Gets things done

Diligent
Hard-working
Industrious
Productive
Efficient

Decent
Gentle
Nice
Polite
Respectful
Courteous
Caring
Concerned
Civil
Generous
Compassionate
Kind

Honest
Open
Straightforward
Trustworthy

Above board

Refined
Sophisticated
Polished
Refined palette
Cosmopolitan
High class
Urbane
Cultured
Well-bred
Well-mannered
Cultivated
Gracious
Mannerly
Smooth
Sociable

Slender
Slim
Trim
Healthy habits
Healthy lifestyle

*Participates in real
    life*
Reads paper books
*Has hobbies and
    interests*
Makes things
Educated

Aware	*Thinks long term*
Literate	
	Stylish
Savvy with finances	*Elegant*
Wise spender	*Well-dressed*
Makes wise choices	*Upscale*

If you have read *Loving Your Epic Small Life*, you will recognize this list and know how I got the idea for it in the first place!

I wrote another recently after spending a period of close-contact time with someone who is a lifelong pessimist and needless worrier. I felt severely drained and depleted from being in their presence, so cleansed my soul with *The Antonym Game*. This list is a nice addition to my earlier list. Here it is!

Confident	*Pleasant*	*Self-aware*
Positive	*Smart*	*Secure*
Bright	*Intelligent*	*At ease*
Cheerful	*Animated*	*Calm*
Optimistic	*Content*	*Certain*
Sunny	*Sparkling*	*Collected*
Encouraging	*Uplifting*	*Composed*
Happy	*Vivacious*	*Cool*
Joyful	*Active*	*Peaceful*
Trusting	*Effervescent*	*Quiet*
Hopeful	*Glad*	*Assured*
Light	*Exciting*	*Tranquil*
Lively	*Interesting*	*Relaxed*
Luminous	*Self-respect*	*Settled*

Agreeable	*Stable*	*Alluring*
Easy-going	*Strong*	*Refreshing*
Refined	*Fit*	*Intriguing*
Upbeat	*Gives praise*	*Lovely*
Enthusiastic	*Thankful*	*Compelling*
Bubbly	*Appreciative*	*Enchanting*
Capable	*Open*	*Playful*
Able	*Self-esteem*	*Entrancing*
Effective	*Attentive*	*Pretty voice*
Useful	*Whimsical*	*Gracious*
Worthwhile	*Glowing*	*Light-*
Competent	*Mindful*	*hearted*
Sound	*A blessing*	*Fascinating*
Healthy	*Productive*	*Spirited*
Hearty	*Attractive*	*Good*
Upright	*Delightful*	*natured*
Independent	*Engaging*	*Energetic*
Resourceful	*Elegant*	*Radiant*

Aren't these *delicious* words? Please don't think I am being unkind by using someone else to do this exercise. I am a spongy, empathetic person who takes on energy from others easily. I find this little exercise not only provides me with an inspiring blueprint on how I want to be, but it also refreshes my spirit.

Reading through my *Who I Am* lists never fails to uplift me and remind me of the elegant lady I desire to me. I hope I have inspired you to try putting together your own, and you don't even have to go through a bad situation to create yours, I hope!

There is an enchanting quality in a person who lives by their values. They seem stable and unshakeable. We are drawn to them without knowing why. We feel safe with them because they come across as sure of themselves and have a strong foundation. They are intriguing because they aren't like other people; we can sense they won't be swayed easily. But we can also see they are good, kind people. It's a charming package for sure.

And the payoff for firstly identifying and then infusing our values into our daily life, is that one day we realize we are living the life of our dreams. Our normal life turned into our 'One day when' life. We're not quite sure how it happened, it just seemed to happen gradually and organically as we got our mind clear on what we wanted. Maybe nothing radical has changed; we still have the same job and husband, but it's just that *we* feel different – happier, more radiant.

How lucky are we that we get to create all of this for ourselves?

Your *Glam Life* tips:

~ Settle in with your journal and make a list of all the **values that are important to you**, and that soothe and calm you. Anything that upsets or irritates you, write down the opposite.

~ **Create your *Who I Am* list** in a similar way, by noting down attractive attributes in yourself and others, favourite words, and things you don't like too so that you can flip it around to the opposite. Then add to this list using a thesaurus. Only write down words that zing you up – leave out any words that 'should' be included but don't cause any kind of reaction for you (or look for a synonym that *does* light you up).

~ To get you started, close your eyes and imagine for a minute **how wonderful it would feel when** your life is X, X and X. For example, in my case, I would infuse the calming feelings of peace, order and simplicity into my body. From this, you can start taking small actions to bring yourself into alignment with your desired feelings. (For my words above this would mean decluttering and organizing, tidying main living spaces, and keeping my schedule not too full).

Your *Glam Life* inspirational questions to contemplate:

~ *What do I value highly?*

~ *Am I living those values right now?*

~ *What small changes could I make in the direction of my values?*

Chapter 15.

Choose a seasonal lifestyle

A simple way to bring more flavour into your life is to begin to live seasonally more often. Almost immediately you can choose to recognize holidays and special days, the four seasons in nature as well as the stage of life you are in right now. Look at the next three months and see what is coming up. What calendar season is it? What time of year? Are there any birthday celebrations or special days in this period?

I find it helps to actually write these things down. I ask myself, 'What month is this?', 'What nature season?' etc. Then I look at simple ways I can be intentional about this time.

When you choose to celebrate little things often, *this* is how you can live your life in the most beautiful and special way. It truly is the secret to a life well-lived. When you do this purposefully, time seems to slow down which is wonderful, because too often another month passes and you don't even know where it went.

Seasons in life

Lean into the rhythms and seasons of life as they come. You can live your life as *big* as you want, but you can't live it all at once and neither would you probably want to.

To best honour your wellbeing and vitality, focus on the season in front of you. Your energy levels will ebb and flow throughout the year. Not expecting yourself to keep going at the same fast pace all the time will help you stay healthy and enjoy things more.

What season are you in right now? Are you at college, studying hard and learning as much as you can? Or are you starting out in your first job? Are you saving for your first home? Have you just started a family? Or perhaps a busy mother in the thick of things? An empty nester? Or a new retiree?

Look at the stage of life you are in objectively and make sure you are not piling too much on yourself. Ponder how you could enjoy it more while still getting everything done. Add in a few fun elements that are a little bit luxurious too. There's no point in slogging it out and saving up all your enjoyment for 'one day' when you are 'less busy'.

I promise you, with that mindset you will never

be less busy. I know this because I am finally figuring it out for myself. I saw that *I have to decide* every day that I'm not too busy for the relaxing things –reading a book, taking a walk outside, or having a nap on a Sunday afternoon – and not too busy to do the things I always said I'd do, such as spending fifteen minutes on some deep stretching.

Take inspiration from others who are in the same stage of life as you – perhaps you know someone who makes everything look a breeze. Breathe in their details and even ask their advice if you know them well enough.

Seasons in nature

The four seasons are another fun way in which to structure your year. Every three months you have a fresh opportunity to adjust what you put on your calendar, subtly update your décor if you so desire, tweak your wardrobe, and change your menu by dining on fresh seasonal produce.

There are loads of ideas on Pinterest on how to live within the four seasons in all sorts of categories: fashion and style, food and drink, and activities. When you're in the mood for a leisurely scroll, instead of social media, research spring, summer, autumn, or winter with a notebook by your side to capture favourite ideas.

Glamour by the seasons

Dream up your favourite ways to add glamour into the seasons. List each season and imagine how you might dress in your ideal life, then let these ideas be the basis for your glamorous seasonal style. Here are a few of mine:

Autumn
Camel coloured clothing with burgundy accessories
Satin blouse in a rich jewel shade
Gold tones in makeup – bronzer, lip gloss

Winter
Faux fur scarf or collar
Tonal dressing
Wearing black with gold jewellery
A fresh red pedicure on moisturized feet

Spring
Highlighted dewy complexion and nude lips
White jeans and a pretty pink top
Wearing floral fragrances

Summer
Dressing 'Riviera Chic' style in stripes, bright colours, and rope wedge sandals
Big sunglasses and a silk scarf worn as a headband
Flowing maxi dresses
Dressing in all white
Bronzed legs

When you're feeling fashion-vibey, it's fun to dream up ways in which you can bring in a little seasonal glamour to elevate your everyday look. You might find you're not so inspired by fashion magazines these days, so doing this lets you make up your own seasonal excitement and inspiration.

Big and little occasions

Big occasions such as weddings, major birthdays and special vacations are all fabulous, but you need the breathing space in between to be able to appreciate them, whether you are the one in charge or merely attending as a guest.

The holidays too, are a big time, so how can you make this time of year easier? More enjoyable? The little details are huge too and can have a lovely grounding, calming effect: I have a Christmas Starbucks mug that I love to drink my tea out of. It really makes me feel cheery and sparkly. Combine this with a Christmas BGM track and I'm the happiest girl around (search for 'Christmas BGM' – which stands for 'background music' on YouTube and you will see what I mean!)

Planning for the next season

I invite you to get a piece of paper and write out a quick and simple outline for the next three months. For some reason, the length of a traditional nature season is an excellent length of time to focus on.

There are many '90-day' action plans on the internet whether you want to lose weight or write a book. Mother nature knew what she was doing when she created one season to be three months long (whether it feels like that where you live or not!)

As I write this chapter it's the month of March, which means it is Autumn here in New Zealand. Our bright summer weather is behind us, and although the days are still beautiful – sunny and bright blue – the evenings are cooler. On my piece of paper I wrote down:

March
Autumn
Cosier recipes
Create a 21-piece capsule wardrobe for Autumn
Change my shoes out for more covered-in styles

I also looked ahead at the next three months: March, April, May, to see if there were any special occasions coming up.

It's my brother's birthday in April, and it just happens to fall on Easter Sunday this year. In the past we have hosted a big Easter Sunday lunch, so I plan to talk to my husband Paul to see if he wants to do it again this year, and have it be my brother's birthday celebration too.

You will find if you do this five-minute exercise as well, that you will feel happy and hopeful about the upcoming season. Even when things can be unpredictable, or should I say *especially* when we

FIONA FERRIS

can't control the happenings of the outside world, it is important to have things to look forward to; little plans to give us hope and feel optimistic.

Create your own fairy tale

When you choose to focus on the season in front of you, whether it's the calendar season, where you are in life, or preparing for a big event, you get to slow down, appreciate where you are, and enjoy it more fully.

I find it also helps with overwhelm, if, for example, you are putting together a big birthday dinner. Most of us don't do those things very often so they can freak us out if we let them. Remind yourself that you can deal with things in the correct season and don't have to do *everything today*. Instead, highly simplify other areas of your life temporarily and fully engage in that occasion.

You will get to enjoy it too, not just your guests, and you will get full value from the money spent. You'll get to look back on that dinner with happy memories rather than recalling the underlying stress you felt.

When you do this with all parts of your life, that's how you can truly feel like you are living in a wonderful fairy tale. Life seems more joyous, easier, more peaceful and calmer. Who wouldn't want to live this kind of dream life?

Your *Glam Life* tip:

If you don't already live your life seasonally, **capture a few ideas that appeal** and see how they fit your style. If they make you feel like things are too complicated drop them, but you might just find a few that enhance your daily experience. And at the very least, you will find that you actually notice the months go by instead of wondering what happened and how did you get to be in another new month without noticing where the last one went!

Your *Glam Life* inspirational questions to contemplate:

~   *What month is it right now?*

~   *What is the nature season?*

~   *What are some of my favourite aspects of this season?*

~   *What would I like to experience in the next three months?*

Chapter 16.
Engage your mind

A beguiling, glamorous lady doesn't just sit around on her sofa watching other people live their lives every night. She certainly *does* watch television series and movies sometimes; they just don't make up one hundred percent of her free time. To keep her days interesting and fun, she has created a life for herself which includes a melange of learning, study, hobbies, passions, and activities. The topics she chooses have nothing to do with her job or career, instead coming from a genuine place of curiosity and play.

She studies things she has always wondered about, reads an intriguing looking dusty old book that she found in a second-hand store, and loves to learn about different periods in history. She feels completer and more rounded when she searches out topics she is interested in rather than having information presented to her by a big media corporation.

She knows it feels wonderful to learn or study something away from her computer screen. When she reads from a page or creates something with her hands, she is being 'in her body' rather than her head, and experiences first-hand how fabulous this is for her mental wellbeing.

Even though it is sometimes not easy to put her phone away for an hour or two, when she does, she can feel her mind relax immediately (even though it is probably throwing a temper tantrum!) She senses her brain working in a different way, a more real way it seems. Doing something physical and 'in the real world' *melts away* any anxiety or vague sense of unease she might be feeling.

Exploring what fascinates her enables her to have her own unique point of view too. Instead of only being plugged into what is popular online, she is following her own intrigue. She enjoys a balance of what is in the zeitgeist and what she chooses for herself. This makes her captivating, not only to others, but to herself as well.

Doesn't this lady sound so intriguing and self-possessed? Like someone you would want to get to know? But then I think, *I'd also have to bring something pretty special to the party.* I'd have to up my game and think about *What can I learn about that I've aways be interested in?* to not just have pedestrian topics to talk with her about.

Wonderful things can happen too. You might start out with the goal to 'engage your mind' and 'be more interesting', but once you really get into something it can take on a life of its own. You could potentially find yourself with a whole new part of your life that is very important to you, that simply never existed before that. You might meet people you never would have had the chance to meet if you hadn't explored the breadcrumbs of interest in a particular subject.

Let's look at what kinds of things we can do to engage our mind. The kinds of things that will make us more *fascinating* and *alluring*, to ourselves and others. Let's turn ourselves on with our own mind. Ooh la la, how delicious!

Here are some of my favourite ideas:

~ **Read a classic book** that has always piqued your interest – many are free on Kindle, or from your library. You can go fiction or non-fiction. I read *The Richest Man in Babylon* many years ago, probably twenty, and it made something click in my head about personal finance. And in terms of novels, I loved *The Great Gatsby* and *Breakfast at Tiffany's*. Both had a glamorous backdrop that made them fun to read! And, it helped that I bought new paperback copies with modern covers. It made them feel fresh and new (to me, a good book cover makes a book more appealing).

~ Study a period of **history in fashion** that has always fascinated you (I love the 1920s and 1930s).

~ Learn about **another period in time** – this interest might be sparked off by a series such as *Downton Abbey* or a movie about Queen Elizabeth I.

~ Choose **a new culinary skill** to learn such as making macarons or hollandaise sauce. Or make your own chutneys.

~ Look at the **curriculum for a finishing school** and see what kinds of topics they offer. You don't necessarily have to enrol with that school, just get ideas from their offerings on what you'd like to study.

~ **Learn a language**. Even if it's just a small amount; you don't have to master the entire language of a country in order to feel like you have learned something.

~ **Watch old movies**. Yes, this is on a screen, but it feels like you are bettering yourself by watching a classic movie such as *Rear Window* or *To Catch a Thief* and not just lying around like a sloth watching trashy reality television! When we have watched an old movie at home it becomes an occasion. We choose the movie, 'book a time' that we are going to watch it, and make an occasion of it, rather than switching on Netflix and scrolling to find something to pass the time.

~ Watch an **art or fashion documentary**. I watched *Very Ralph* (about Ralph Lauren) recently and it was so inspiring to go after your dreams, dress well, and be creative. I also have a collection of French art documentaries which give me a fascinating insight not only into another time, but also the mind of an artist.

~ Learn how to sew, knit or crochet, or **revive your interest in a craft**. Upcycle clothes. Design your own. Learn how to make patterns.

~ **Study floral art**. There are beautiful books around which show you how to create a display, whether you prefer traditional or modern styles. Learn how to use materials from your own garden.

~ Learn a specific **dance such as salsa or the tango**. Find out the mindset and history behind the dance and really get your whole being on board: body, soul and mind.

Start a journal page with your notes on what appeals, what you'd like to learn about in the future, and keep it as a place to record those little sparks of interest.

It will be a place to bank your ideas for now and the future. Be excited for all the fun activities and hobbies that are available to you. There really is no limit to what you can learn and achieve.

Give yourself permission to follow what piques your interest and gather together all the things you enjoy thinking about and doing. When you do this, not only will you make yourself a very good life, you will also live a life that is curated to be exactly 'you'.

Nothing is ever wasted. No effort or time you put towards your dream life will ever be for nothing, because it all builds upon itself. And even if the future isn't exactly what you planned for, you've still had fun along the way, and it will continue to get better and better. It is a much nicer feeling to have fun plans and put one foot in front of the other while you explore them rather than thinking, *When I get 'there' it will be* good.

Deep down we already know that *Life is good now, very good,* and it will *continue* to be if we let it. We are not putting off fabulous times until the future but *living them now*. And having a fantastic time in the future too, whether it's in five years' time or at retirement. Our goodness compounds and it's fantastic.

Give yourself the gift of following what lights you up and be that desirable lady who is living her life in her own style. It is available to you, to all of us. Why wouldn't we accept this incredible gift!

Your *Glam Life* tips:

~   How will you **add glamour to your life by engaging your mind**? Will you create art? Express yourself through the written word? Or study fashion? The more you explore, the more you will find.

~   Keep a running list of **topics that interest you** and add to it as you come across more. Read through your list regularly and let ideas present themselves to you. There is no need to force anything.

~   **Ask people more interesting questions** and pick up on cues as to what they have been up to lately. Show a genuine interest; it's easy to do this when you are also engaging your mind in ways that are outside the popular culture psyche.

Your *Glam Life* inspirational questions to contemplate:

~ *What did I love to learn or read about as a child?*

~ *What hobbies did I love to play around with?*

~ *Is there something I've always wondered about but never made a move with such as ballroom dancing or tango?*

~ *What one thing would I like to pursue right now?*

Chapter 17.
Dine luxuriously

Imagine walking into a cooler-than-cool place such as the iconic Hôtel Costes in Paris. You're dressed as your next-level self and feel amazing. The music is sexy and fabulous. You're part of the scene! No, scratch that, you *are* the scene. You're walking slow-motion like in a movie, people are turning to look at you, and you *own the room.*

When you are in this state of mind is how you can uplevel your palate and choose to be a lady who dines luxuriously. Junky low-rent foods hold no power over you anymore. You are first-class all the way.

But just how can we bring a level of luxury into our everyday meals, when we still have to get to work, look after the family and pets – and ourselves! How can we make it easy for ourselves to dine luxuriously on a day-to-day basis. Well I'm so glad you asked. I have a few thoughts, and not all of them are flossy; some are very practical in fact!

Run your kitchen like a restaurant

See? I told you they're practical! What I've worked out is that it's the behind-the-scenes that makes a place successful. This counts for a business such as a hotel, restaurant, bar or even a retail store, but it also applies to us in our home. When good systems are in place it's easier to have peace and ease when getting a meal on the table, and not only will you dine in a more luxurious manner, but you will save money too.

I love watching *Gordon Ramsay's Kitchen Nightmares* on television – I know, not very chic of me! – but I can see just as quickly as Gordon why a place isn't doing well. Their fridge is overstocked with gross, old food. They don't manage their stock well. The menu has a million items on it. The dining room looks tired and the staff uninspired.

It's fun to see Gordon whip everything into shape. He trims the menu and trains the kitchen how to master a smaller number of dishes. He cleans out spoiled food and gives the entire kitchen a scrub down. He puts systems into place such as fresh foods stacked up in clear containers with dates written on tape, so staff know which is the older stock and which is newer. He gives everyone a pep talk – employees and owners alike. The dining room is refreshed on a minimal budget.

These are all things we can do in our own home to bring back the enjoyment of cooking meals for our family. Or create enthusiasm if we never enjoyed it to start with!

Keep Gordon Ramsay in mind if you are feeling flat and dull about your kitchen, and cooking in general. Give your kitchen a jolly good clean. Clear out your cabinets of small appliances and food prep gadgets that you just never use. Even if you don't donate them straight away, put them all into a box and store them elsewhere temporarily just so you can get the motivating and satisfying feeling of a kitchen that has space to *breathe* in.

Go through your fridge, freezer and pantry and take out expired foods or items you always pass over. I threw out a handful of jars from my fridge recently – a jar of pâté I had been given (I don't like pâté and didn't know how long you could keep it for once it had been opened), some expired green curry paste that I hadn't used in a long time, and a few other things that had sat there waiting for me to magically want to use them. I kept them out of guilt for wasting food but can I tell you, when I gave myself permission to only have items in my fridge that made me happy to see them, it felt *amazing*. I felt light as air!

And it also gave me the desire to use up other items and zing up my meals. Previously they had been stored among jars that I didn't want to go near, so I didn't 'see' them.

Stage a pretty dining table

It's the same with your dining area. Make it an appealing place to be. Think how a staff member would set up a table at Hôtel Costes. They would start with a tablecloth, or placemats for a more casual look. Add salt and pepper grinders then a candle, or flower in a bud vase. Choose napkins that complement the table setting or perhaps the season.

It's so enjoyable to set an elegant table when you have guests over, and lovely for a family dinner too. And, when you have your table set, even if partially, other family members won't be so quick to use the dining table as a dumping ground.

A touch I like to add is to put the dinner plate at each table setting, just like in a glossy magazine layout. I used to stack plates by the food area for guests to serve themselves but always preferred the look of plates set at the table.

Then I realized that people need somewhere to put their drink so they can get dinner. This works perfectly because they claim their spot, place their drink down, and take their plate away. The next person sees the places that are still available and the dinner traffic flows smoothly!

Create an appealing menu

Restaurants have a menu too, for customers to order from. So plan your meals, even if loosely. I wish I loved doing the full menu planning thing but it feels too restrictive to me, so instead I do it 'my way'. I make sure I have enough fresh produce for at least the next few night's meals. I can pull something out of the freezer and add vegetables from the fridge and dinner will be served that night.

What will you have on your menu? Instead of thinking, *We 'should' be a bit healthier, let's get some veggies*, go for the thought of *lusciously healthy fresh and nutritious food* – food that promotes beauty. Good nutrition makes your skin prettier!

Water-rich foods for a vibrant and juicy hydrated complexion

Good fats such as avocado, olive oil and raw nuts for happy, vivacious cells

Protein from a source of your choice to keep you active and satiated throughout your day

There are so many ways we can sell ourselves on healthy food when we reframe it as glamorous, beauty-enhancing and being an all-round more attractive person who is living their best life with high energy and feel-good happiness.

If you lead a busy life

But what about if you have a killer schedule and you buy quick and easy fast food or other options that you know aren't the healthiest choice but just can't see any other way?

I have seen pre-prepared components to a meal around more now, such as washed and sliced vegetables, ready-cooked meats, and salads in a bag with little sachets of yummy toppings and the dressing ready to mix through. I buy these occasionally to supplement a meal but mostly make my own.

However, when I am strapped for time, I purchase these items, and while the cost is more than a DIY salad for example, is still less expensive than dining out or going through the drive through. From what I've seen, even fast food is expensive these days, and the portions have shrunk too! When we were at the airport recently my husband bought a well-known hamburger meal and I couldn't believe how small it was. Even the bun size had shrunk. He had to buy two burgers to feel full.

It's just more luxurious and glamorous to eat real food, whether it's partially prepared or you do it yourself from scratch. I have been using reverse psychology on myself for so long now that fast food mostly looks gross and unappealing instead of calling a siren song to me like it used to.

Spin an aura of glamour around you and your kitchen and decide that you are ready to be a high-maintenance lady who wouldn't let anything sub-par pass her lips. She wouldn't want anything to smudge her lip gloss! She clinks her elegant glass with you and sips her mineral water delicately as she lifts a fork to start her elegant and health-enhancing dinner. *Bon Appétit*, she says!

Your *Glam Life* tips:

~ **Invite Gordon into your kitchen** and see what he'd do. Is he going to pull open an overflowing drawer of utensils and ask you to sort through them? Perhaps get you to make your dining area a more inviting place to be? Channel him and see what he says!

~ Make over your kitchen and have it **be a luxurious place** that you can't wait to cook in. Declutter anything in it that brings about feelings of guilt or that just doesn't feel like the next-level you; anything that is where you have been in the past, not where you are heading to now.

~ **Uplevel your palate** and become someone who is very particular with what she eats. By eating more healthful and water-rich foods, you will begin to crave them more. Be that elegant lady.

Your Glam Life inspirational questions to contemplate:

~ *How can I upgrade my dining experience? What area am I going to begin with?*

~ *What is the hotel or restaurant I am going to keep in mind as my dining muse?*

~ *How can I enchant myself as I dine? Is it the lighting, music, and candles? The table setting? What is the vibe I am going for?*

~ *How can I make it fun and easy to elevate how I eat? What motivates me?*

Chapter 18.
Be wealthy in all ways

Rich = glamorous, but not necessarily in the way you might think. You don't need a private jet or matching Gucci luggage to play the part. Instead, why not be one of those unicorn people who live 'richer' than their paycheck suggests and become wealthy immediately? I'm sure you know at least one person like this. They live very well on their normal-person income. You know they don't carry crazy levels of debt. In fact, you wonder how they can have such an easy time with money!

I'm here to let you in on a little secret. It is possible to be savvy with money and live well 'beyond your means'. You don't need to be born rich. Anyone with intention can improve on where they are at.

You might wonder why, when you have a

reasonable income, certainly not that different from friends, family and colleagues, do you always seem to be chasing your tail? Getting to the next pay day and having your money go out the door once again and you find you're waiting for the next payday.

For me I found it was because I was spending indiscriminately on things that were not important to me. I had many leaks in my money bucket, so no matter that my pay went in regularly to fill it up, it was leaking out everywhere! It is *not glamorous* to be broke from poor spending habits.

Be inspired by people who live well on modest incomes

What do they know that we don't? The main factor in my view, is that they extract the most juice from their spending as possible. They look at all their expenditures to see if they are getting the most value. They want to use their incoming funds to good effect and gain as much from their money as they can.

Their spending aligns with what they find most important – as detailed in *Chapter 14. Live by your values.* They will spend when they esteem something and save when they don't. Learn from them by spending your money on things that are meaningful to you and not on things that don't fill you up.

Look at recurring payments too; a lot of damage can be done there without you realizing, even when the numbers are small. Take a weekly or monthly amount and multiply it to get an annual figure. This may shock you into action!

In addition, consider whether the money you spend is leading you towards your ideal life or away from it? In my case, I saw that the money I spent on snack foods each week really added up over time, *and* was not enhancing my goal of being slim and healthy. You can move towards two goals at the same time.

The aim is not to make yourself miserable by cutting out everything you find enjoyable. The aim is to have the most fun possible while spending the least. Cut out the dead wood I say!

It's just like decluttering your closet

Say you have fifty items hanging in your wardrobe for the current season. You only wear a small percentage of them on a regular basis because many of the items have something not quite right about them. A couple have fabric which is scratchy against your skin. This one has a low neckline so you always have to wear a camisole under it but that never feels quite 'you'. This one clings to your muffin-top and looks awful. And this one, well the colour of it drains all the blood from your face and you look sick!

When you take those fifty items and go through them one by one, only putting back the pieces that fit you, you feel comfortable in, they look good on you, and you aren't constantly adjusting, you might be left with only nineteen pieces. But, you love those nineteen pieces! You would happily wear any one of them today. You look at the rest that are piled up on your bed and you decide that they are not good enough for you. They make you feel bad. And you aren't going to retrieve any of the money spent by leaving them in your closet. So you donate them. And you've never been happier to get dressed in the morning. Plus, you feel like you have more options, not less. It's magical!

That's how it is with your spending. When you take it all out of your spending closet and look at the fit of it, you'll see that when you put back only the spending that makes you feel the happiest and gives you true pleasure (which feels good afterwards, versus false pleasure which gives you a slightly queasy feeling the next day), you will radically trim your spending without sacrificing anything.

The main culprits I find, as already mentioned, are recurring costs. Magazine and streaming subscriptions. Once-a-year payments that seem hard to cancel so you let them go by for another year. I had a *Dropbox* payment for a service that I didn't even really need, and it went out. I was so annoyed with myself, but I made sure to cancel it before the next annual payment. And auto-renewal on magazines are the devil's work as far as I'm concerned! Put reminders in your phone's calendar a month before. Do this when you trial something for free as well, so that you can cancel it before the payments start if you don't want to carry on with it.

It depends on the financial season of life you are in as well. When my husband and I were saving for our first home and then focused on paying it off quickly (as detailed in my book *Financially Chic: Live a luxurious life on a budget, learn to love managing money, and grow your wealth*), we spent just about nothing beyond the basics. We made our own cheap fun.

But now, fifteen years on, we have been able to free up the purse strings. Currently we pay for four different streaming services. The monthly fees are reasonable for what you get and we enjoy the selection. But we were talking about it recently and said that if we were starting out again, we wouldn't have any, no matter how inexpensive, because there is still plenty of free-to-air and on-demand content to watch.

I don't need to buy expensive things, but I do love convenience. We'll get meal kit boxes when they send us a special offer, I send my husband's business shirts out to get laundered, and we have cleaners once a week to make our home lovely. But if we were in a different financial stage of our lives, we would have none of those things.

Dave Ramsay says to 'live like no-one else today so you can live like no-one else tomorrow'. This is what we've done. We lived like no-one else back then (we were far more thrifty than any of our family and friends), so we can live like no-one else today (our house is paid off, we have investments, I get to stay at home as an author/happy housewife, and we can spend a little more having fun than we used to).

Make more money with a side hustle

When blogs first came out I started my own and loved writing on it, because I had always wanted to be a writer. With my blog I could connect with other like-minded ladies and share my inspiration. But I still desired to be an author, a proper author who wrote books; it was just that I didn't know how to make this happen. It all seemed too hard.

Then, when I started to see other bloggers self-publishing, I became excited by the possibility and took the first steps to do this in 2015. Back then, I worked full-time and wrote before work and on the weekends. Now, it's my full-time income and I don't have to go to work at all. Having fun and playing around with ideas *is* my work. (I wrote a book about how I did this, it's called *The Chic Author: Create your dream career and lifestyle, writing and self-publishing non-fiction books*).

You might want to be a writer too. Or sell handmade or digital items on Etsy. You can open your own eStore and sell to the world or start a YouTube channel and share your views on your favourite topics. Maybe you'll offer one-on-one coaching or fashion stylist sessions via Zoom or Skype. You can earn a little or a lot from your own creativity, hobbies, passions, and interests. It doesn't even matter if you are a homebody introvert. I am too!

What matters is that you take the first, tiny step. Make a list of ideas that appeal. See what other people you follow online are doing and ask yourself if you would like to do that too. For me, writing books is so much fun and it suits my personality. Turning up live on YouTube seems like a lot of effort and terrifying too! But pottering away with my ideas and dreams on paper and uploading my books to Amazon for anyone to read if they want to and not if they don't, feels full of ease. I don't have to sell myself to anyone. If someone doesn't like my books, they will find another author who resonates with them more. I am here for the readers who want *me*.

But for others, writing a book is a huge mountainous task. They wouldn't know where to start. And jumping on YouTube to do a live video is easy and fun for them. One lady I know whose videos are enjoyable and educational for me to watch earns millions a year from her channel and video courses she offers. And she started out from zero too. I'm not earning millions a year but I love that I get to earn what would be considered a good income where I live. I'm very happy with that, and I don't even have to go to work. How awesome is that!

Don't think I'm special, because I'm not. I just decided to try something out and see what happened. Like Dave Ramsay said, I decided to live like no-one else today, so I could live like no-one else tomorrow. I got up an hour earlier and wrote for that hour each day before work. And now, seven years later, I still do the same. I love waking up early! I do my writing before my day starts and then the day is my own.

Start a side hustle and have fun with it. It can only lead to good things!

Your *Glam Life* tips:

~ **Decide to change your mindset** around money. Become someone who looks at money as something fun, easy and playful. It's possible to change how you feel about money. I know because I did it!

~ **Declutter your expenditures**. Write down your values and see if they align with how you spend your money.

~ **Choose to lead a rich life**. Fill yourself up with experiences and good relationships and don't just rely on money for fun. So many outings cost very little and will enhance your life immensely. Having friends around for afternoon tea. Dressing up and going for a walk around the city on the weekend. Hosting your neighbours for dinner. Having your own spa day at home on a Sunday. At the risk of promoting yet a third book of mine in the one chapter, my book *100 Ways to Live a Luxurious Life on a Budget* is a 'wealth' of knowledge on living well without spending a lot of money.

Your *Glam Life* inspirational questions to contemplate:

~   *What do I value most? (Search online for a 'list of values' if you are stuck. Then keep these words in mind to help you decide what to spend money on and what not to.)*

~   *If I had a side hustle, what could it be? What am I interested in? What am I good at? What might people pay me for?*

~   *How can I get the most from my current paycheck? Is there 'dead wood' I can cut out painlessly in order to free up cash to put towards things I really desire?*

Chapter 19.

Adopt an apology-free lifestyle

Have you been covering yourself up? Hiding your authentic, true self under layers of what you consider to be acceptable to others? Afraid to show the real you in case people reject you? Or worrying that there is something fundamentally unlikable about you?

Yeah, me too, and it's exhausting. So debilitating. And it doesn't even work! You know you're tip toeing around. People can sense that you're not presenting honestly. Perhaps you are in some areas, but not in others. You worry that they will shun you completely if they know what you're really like.

Well guess what, none of this will happen. Not even a little bit. And if it does, they are not your people! But let's back up, there is no need to come out like a contestant on a makeover show and say, *Ta da! Here I am!* No, we don't need to be that dramatic (or do we...? It *would* be epic). Perhaps we can do that in our mind, just for fun. And be more low-key as we step into our apology-free lifestyle.

For most of us, it can be a happy time of self-exploration to uncover *what we really like*. And start being, doing and having those things. We can do it little steps at a time, with the occasional quantum leap, and creatively shape our future to be everything we've ever dreamed of.

Please yourself

Maybe, like me, you've been a people pleaser for a long time. You look to make people comfortable, and may even consider them before you consider yourself. You make decisions based on what other people want. You go along with what others want to do. It seems like a reasonable thing to do, otherwise you'd be a selfish person, right? It's better to be a nice person who doesn't rock the boat or make other people uncomfortable by speaking up.

But what happens when you do this consistently? I'll tell you how it felt for me. You exhaust yourself and become burnt out. Resentful. Unhappy and grumpy. And all from something of your own making! No-one was asking you to be like this, you just... ended up being like it.

Once I found out I had a choice, and actually, it was better for me to be how I wanted to be, love what I loved, and live how I wanted to live, my life started to unfold in beautiful ways.

There is something truly liberating that happens when you really own yourself. When you speak up for what you want. Live in your truth. You don't need to hurt others either, that's not what happens. What does happen though, is that others will respect you more. Be drawn to you, and like you more.

This is what happens when you live your best life *without apology*. When you own what you love *without apology*.

If you love shopping, wealth, and glamour, there is no need to feel bad about that (people say it's frivolous).

If you love a quiet and simple life with plenty of free time in your schedule and space to potter and play at home, own that (people say you never go anywhere).

If you decide to change the way you eat to support your healthy lifestyle goals, you get to do that with pleasure (people say you're boring and never eat anything fun).

And if you decide to change your mind about anything at any time, that's fine too. Be a homebody one day and plan an overseas trip the next. Be a chic fashionista one day and a stylish minimalist the next. Eat snack foods one day and eat cleanly the next. You get to change if and when you want to. You do not owe anyone an explanation.

You wouldn't put someone out on purpose, but there is no need to go through every single nuance of your decision-making process if you want to do something differently, nor have to justify it to them. You simply get to live your life in a way that makes you happy.

When you say sorry as a habit

This is so common and I used to do it too (and probably still do more than is necessary). But you will come across so much better, and feel better in yourself when you don't say sorry to others all the time. Learn how to *not* say sorry for every little thing. Living your best most glamorous life means not being a doormat!

Sorry I'm making you uncomfortable by choosing this for myself
Sorry because you bumped into me in a store
Sorry I'm not willing to go along with your plans because they will impact mine
Sorry I can't make your problem my problem

You can still be kind without saying sorry all the time. You can still be a caring person who considers the comfort of others. You're just getting rid of that default, 'Oh sorry' every five minutes. Once you start doing this, you will notice how often some people do say it. And it doesn't come across well! It's a balancing act, definitely. Especially to start with.

Live life on your own terms

The alternative to all of this is making intentional decisions on how you want to live, ensuring they are in alignment with your true desires, and not feeling like you have to sell your plans on anyone but yourself. You will inspire others when you do this.

They will see you living a good life, having fun, and choosing the flavour of your lifestyle. When you live in the manner you desire, others feel like they can do the same. When you do something outside of the norm, it gives people permission to follow their dreams too.

Having children didn't work out for my husband and I, and we decided to have it be the making of us. We decided it was the best thing that could have happened to us, even though I know we would have loved being parents too. And it was the making of us! We have lived a wonderful life so far and have fun plans for our future as well.

At the time when we were trying for a family, I know there were people who thought we should have tried harder, done more, gone further with medical treatment. But we didn't want to, so we didn't. It was important at the time to keep our own vision in mind and not feel dragged down by what other people thought was best for us.

When you think about it objectively, what is a good reason for being apologetic for wanting something different in life (something that other people wouldn't even probably give a second thought to). Yet that's what many of us do. We live our life for others and then wonder why we feel so unhappy about our choices from time to time.

Take back the reins. You are the one in the driving seat of your life, no-one else. You don't have to be aggressive about it, just make a decision that you are the one in charge. You get to choose. And from that point on, own your desires without apology. Maybe you will start out a little softer by observing where you defer to others needlessly.

Start taking small steps such as what you'd like for dinner, and what music you feel like listening to. Dress in something you really want to wear in the morning. Choose your attitude for the day and wear it happily (maybe Cheery and Productive? Or Relaxed and Goddess-like?)

Enjoy every minute of your glam life by choosing yourself. You will love it!

Your Glam Life tips:

~ **Inspire others by your example** of making intentional decisions on how you want to live. Be unapologetically glam! How much fun does that sound?

~ Remember that **you get to choose** what you want, and you can change your mind too if you want to.

~ **Hop into the driver's seat**! Don't just be someone who drifts through life not really knowing what they want. Ask yourself who you want to be and *be that girl*!

Your Glam Life inspirational questions to contemplate:

~ *In what areas have I been apologizing, perhaps for a long time? (I know for me, I've been apologizing internally for being a curvy girl, not skinnier. And for no reason, no-one is asking me about it. From now on, I am me, just me. I can focus on health, not being thinner.)*

~ *Who might be most upset if I started changing? Are they important in my life? If so, how can I begin to evolve in a way that doesn't alienate them? Can I bring them along on my journey by talking about little snippets of my fun plans after I have started implementing them?*

~ *How does my future life look in my dreams? How can I step into it now?*

Chapter 20.
Your glam life starts now

Here's a fun little project for you: try a pair of polarized sunglasses on and see how they make everything look better. The sky will look different – there is greater contrast – the clouds are whiter, and the sky is bluer. The colour of the grass and trees are brighter, greener. When you take the sunglasses off, by comparison everything will seem less vibrant. Move them up and down and see how your world is brighter, duller, brighter, duller.

This is how you can begin your glam life today: You can apply this same filter to how you live your life and choose the flavour of your filter too. It's not making things up, because everything you see through your sunglasses is real. It's just that now your view is enhanced. It is more enticing, magnetizing, and appealing. You enjoy it more because it *looks so good* in comparison.

We can take things a step further too: we can apply this same beguiling filter to everything we do, using all of our *senses* and our *mind*, not just our eyes. Many of the ways you can do this you will already be doing, but you can amp it up even more.

Your glam life starts today. *It starts every day.* Don't let another week go by being the same old person living the same dull life. Even if you think life is fun and amazing (I certainly do) it can still get even better. You get to choose!

Here's how you can do it. Here's how you can live your glam life today, and every day. Become someone who:

~   Looks for the positive as much as possible.

~   Talks *everything* up.

~   Chooses beauty to surround herself with.

~   Endeavours to be a bright ray of sunshine every day.

~   Applies a golden-rose filter to how she views things.

~   Elevates all areas in her life with a dash of glamour.

~   Ignites all her senses – she actually goes

through them and sees that she is enhancing her experience in each area: What's in her line of vision, check! What she hears, check! The scents around her, check! How something feels on her skin, check! The tastes she treats herself to, check! And the thoughts in her mind – they are positive and uplifting. Check!

~ Goes through her schedule: Where she spends her time, who she is with and how she is dressed and *makes it even more special*. She takes it over the top, in a good way.

~ Acts in alignment with her ideal self. When something feels a little off, she finds out why and sorts it. She keeps her peace of mind this way.

~ Chooses the glamour route and is happy to expend that little bit more effort because she knows it's worth it.

Sometimes the glamour route *does* take more effort. Remember, if it was easy everyone would be doing it. Don't be average and your life won't be average. *You* are next-level. Not everyone can have your glamorous life and of course not everyone will want it, but you do. You love to enjoy your daily life and you let yourself do that in perhaps an unconventional way.

Let glamour surround you

Setting your environment up for success is such a fun thing to do. On a normal day elevate yourself by dressing in your nicest clothes (which are still appropriate for what you have planned). Wear perfume, spend an extra five minutes making your hair look good, and paint your nails. Tidy up the space around you, light a candle, turn on soft background music and switch on table lamps. Even if it's just you at home.

Create your own flavour of filter too. Channel a feeling ('sparkle', 'peacefulness' or 'elegance'), a person (for me Aerin Lauder, a character in a favourite movie, or Martha Stewart), or a place (perhaps Paris, California, or a tropical resort), and let it guide you. It's much better than having a to-do list, and less effort too. You will find that you get all the things done that you need to without thinking about them too much. You will get great results, and you will enjoy yourself more as well.

That's the small daily details but take it to the bigger things too. When you are decluttering and organizing, think about the vision you have for the room you are in. How could you make it next-level fabulous? Even without buying anything new?

When I think about this for myself it is being extra ruthless with removing clutter, making everything extra clean, and perhaps moving in a few unexpected décor touches from other rooms. Being a little over the top and theatrical. Making everything extra special.

And when you do need to buy something new, whether it's bedroom furniture or a few new tops for winter, let your filter help you choose too. Let glamour lead the way and see what she shows you. It might be a bit much for you as you are right now, but then again you might be thrilled with what she has chosen. Those little mini-upgrades to the ideal self you have in mind are so thrilling to step into. They really add a *frisson* to daily living.

When you have a filter, whether it's for the day, a project, or your whole year (like the word-of-the-year idea), it suddenly becomes clear just what your priorities and necessary actions are, without you having to effort at all. You are instantly crystal clear!

Your Glam Life tips:

~ **Start your glam life today**, and every day! Life really is what you make of it, so make it everything you've ever dreamed of. Collect ideas in your preferred medium (a journal, Pinterest, voice recordings or a vision board) and build a picture for yourself. Infuse your life with details that light you up.

~ **Become someone who sparkles**. You are lit from within. Be excited for your wonderful life!

50 Ways to live your most glamorous life

You didn't think I'd leave you hanging, without a final inspirational boost did you? As you might have seen in many of my other books, I love to end with a list, and not just any list. A list that inspires action, that lifts you up and places you on a cloud floating far above the everyday humdrum of life.

Please enjoy my final bonus chapter on fifty ways to live your most glamorous life!

1. *You are a glamourista*. Reside in a **glamorous state of mind** always.

2. Be **divinely feminine** in everything you do. Move slower, talk less, be soft in your body.

3. **Pamper your skin** and treat it well for a glowing complexion.

4. Wear **twice as much mascara** as you think you need.

5. Have a beautiful vision for your life and refer back to it often. Think of it as your own **glamour manifesto**.

6. **Embody goddess energy** as you walk and see how you sway.

7. Simplify your home space to **make room for your ideal life**.

8. **Be on vacation in your mind** as you go about your tasks – feel the warm ocean breeze on your skin!

9. **Glam up an area of your life** that feels unsatisfying to you right now.

10. Make **healthy habits your top priority** to become 'that girl'.

11. Choose to **live life on your own terms**. Decide what your favourite flavour is and own it, unapologetically.

12. When you travel, dress exquisitely. **Pretend you are in a movie**. Put on your big sunglasses and drape a pashmina around your shoulders.

13. **Embody elegance** when you dine.

14. Become the most **confident person** you know.

15. Have one or two sets of **exquisite bed sheets** instead of multiple cheap sets.

16. **Dress for your dream life**, not the one you have right now. Step into the next-level you via your closet.

17. Choose to **live a life of glamour** rather than what everyone else does. Find fun ways in which to do this.

18. Become **supremely organized** so you can move through life unencumbered.

19. **Do nice things for yourself** as often as you can.

20. Dress well **no matter your budget**.

21. Bring **a cheery, sparky attitude** to everything you do. Be that positive lady.

22. Reframe exercise to be something you look forward to by considering it an **essential part of any successful glamourista's lifestyle**.

23. Dedicate time to **tend to your nails** every week, whether you prefer them neatly buffed, or glossy red.

24. **Have fabulous hair**. Spend the time to wash and style it and learn how to make the most of your hair.

25. Every so often dedicate a whole day just to you and **do exactly as you please**.

26. Become **best friends with your iron** and wear beautifully pressed clothes. Also snip off loose threads, and use a pilling shaver when necessary.

27. Wear one **wow-factor accessory** at all times, such as an oversized watch, huge amazing sunglasses, or chandelier earrings. 'Tasteful, yet striking' is the vibe you're after.

28. Cultivate exquisite posture by imagining **a silken thread drawing you up** from the top of your head.

29. Practice being emotionally stable. **Exude calm confidence** in any situation.

30. **Dress up more**: decide to amp everything up – whether it's by 10% or 100% is up to you.

31. Look at putting makeup on as **a little piece of art** that you get to do every day, no matter if you wear a tiny smidge or the smokiest of eyes.

32. **Make glamour a must**. Just decide it is how you are going to live from now on, and so it will be.

33. Speak up for yourself if needed, in **a cool and poised manner**.

34. **Never criticize** or put yourself down, whether you are around others or alone.

35. **Give yourself pep talks**, daily even. Write them down if this works better for you. Tell yourself how well you are doing and to keep on going!

36. It's an oldie but a goodie: 'If you can't say anything nice, don't say anything at all'. Become known as the lady who **always has positive things to say**.

37. Think about the **first impression** you want to make and dress from that place.

38. Make a list of things you might do in your **idealistic glamorous lifestyle** and do those things more.

39. Surround yourself with **symbols of your glamorous life**, both big and small. Think glossy coffee table books, a clean and tidy space, gold accessories and fresh or silk flowers.

40. Enjoy being **high-maintenance**. Decide that low-maintenance is no longer where you're at even though once upon a time you wore it proudly.

41. Have your first cup of tea or coffee **in bed in the morning** like a diva. Prop pillows up behind you and read an inspiring book or write from your future self in your journal (ask for her advice!)

42. Create or find a playlist on Spotify or similar which evokes **a feeling of glamour** for you, whether it's old Hollywood, or sultry and European.

43. **Make the most of your natural assets** (aka your body) by looking after her well, such as regular dental appointments, nourishing meals, hydrating with water, long showers with quality products, moisturizer all over, early nights and beautifully positive thoughts.

44. Wear **matte lipstick** in red, soft plum, or melon.

45. Think before you speak, and speak clearly and slowly. Lower your voice a little and **let people receive your words easily**.

46. Whether you drink Champagne or not, keep it in mind as **a symbol to emulate**: softly bubbly, luxurious, expensive, not easily available to everyone, and highly desirable. You are exclusive, elegant, and evocative.

47. Pack your life with **so many mesmerizing things** that there is no room for grumbles.

48. **Choose a style icon** (perhaps from another era) and have her be your glamorous chic mentor. Ask yourself, *What would she do? How would she dress? What would she eat?*

49. **Cultivate a taste for stylish foods** that other, less glamorous creatures might say, *Ooh yuck, no thanks* to, such as olives, black coffee and persimmons.

50. **Remember the star that you are**. You are the lead character in your own show! Act the part, enjoy it, and dress for it. Play your role with sparkling confidence and enjoy every minute of your performance!

Sparkle from the inside out

My final reminder to you is to let your glam life spill out without you speaking about it. There is no need to, it will all be communicated with how you are *being* instead. Maybe you have a like-minded friend you'll want to chat with about the effervescent filter you've chosen, but I wouldn't even advise that to start with.

I have found that when I share my fanciful and beautiful mind confetti with someone because I just couldn't hold in the goodness any longer, they didn't get it. And how could they? They haven't been building it up in their mind like I have.

Instead, I have found it far better to create my own inner world to illuminate my life. In my mind there are pretty dust motes floating around as the sun streams through my filter. You can be truly happy when you create your own dreamworld. Life can be a fairy tale if you want it to be. Having a happy mind will help you deal with stress and enjoy your work more.

People won't know quite what is different about you; they can't put their finger on it, but they know there is something. You are captivating to them and they want to be around you. You won't have to search for friendship or company, it will come to you.

Yes you, the fabulous creature like no other who is simply having fun living her life, making it as good as it can be. And the best thing is, you are enjoying yourself more than you ever have. You are creating your life exactly as you desire to live it. You are living the dream. You are an inspiration to those around you. You lift them up by your example. They can't wait to see what you do next, and you notice they are elevating themselves also.

Enjoy the butterfly effect you are creating and please be sure to let me know how you get on. I would be beyond grateful if you would leave me a review on Amazon. I read all my reviews (Amazon sends me notifications) and it gives me happy goosebumps to hear of your successes and ideas.

When I read reviews for other books I love to receive snippets of inspiration, so please, when you write a review for *The Glam Life*, include details of what you've done as a result of reading this book. Or maybe your plans and dreams. Document them there! Imagine coming back to that review a year later and seeing how your life has changed simply as a result of claiming *your glam life*. Reviews don't have to be long, but they can be if you want to!

And, if you'd like to be notified about my new releases, click the Follow button on my Amazon author page here:

Amazon.com/author/fionaferris

It is my sincere hope that you enjoyed this book and now have many new ideas. Remember, the main thing is to do what makes you happy. Fill yourself up with uplifting thoughts and desires and soon your overflow will bless those around you.

Be that person who inspires others by the way she lives and you will be providing a much needed service at the same time as tap-dancing your way through life.

I wish you all the fantastical and luminous luck in the world as you filter your life through glamour. I'm raising a virtual flute with something pretty and bubbly in it to you. Here's cheers to your wonderful and fun life. You are amazing!

With fond thanks,

xx Fiona

About the author

Fiona Ferris is passionate about and has studied the topic of living well for more than twenty years, in particular that a simple and beautiful life can be achieved without spending a lot of money.

Fiona finds inspiration from all over the place including Paris and France, the countryside, big cities, fancy hotels, music, beautiful scents, magazines, books, all those fabulous blogs out there, people, pets, nature, other countries and cultures; really, everywhere she looks.

Fiona lives in the beautiful and sunny wine region of Hawke's Bay, New Zealand, with her husband, Paul, their rescue cats Jessica and Nina and rescue dogs Daphne and Chloe.

To read more of Fiona's books, you can find her at:

amazon.com/author/fionaferris

Or search online for: *Fiona Ferris books*

You can also connect with Fiona here:

howtobechic.com
fionaferris.com
facebook.com/fionaferrisauthor
twitter.com/fiona_ferris
instagram.com/fionaferrisnz
youtube.com/fionaferris

Printed in Great Britain
by Amazon

11636371R00103